# A Penguin Special
## *CRISIS OVER CRUISE*

Barry Rubin, Philip Webber and ~~Graeme Wilkinson~~ are the authors of *London After the Bomb* ( ~~    ~~ ~~    ~~ ) ~~    ~~ ~~    ~~ ~~    ~~ about nuclear arms and believe that on issues such as these, scientists have a special responsibility to society. They have all been closely involved in the current nuclear debate – participating in various TV and radio programmes – and have acted as advisers to many organizations, including the Greater London Council, the BMA, the BBC, and the Royal Shakespeare Company, as well as CND and many other peace groups. On behalf of Scientists Against Nuclear Arms, Philip Webber and Graeme Wilkinson have helped produce briefing documents on Cruise and other topics for MPs.

Barry Rubin gained his BA in chemistry and PhD in physical chemistry at the University of Pennsylvania. From 1969 to 1972 he held Research Fellowships at Bristol University, and at Northwestern University, USA, then at Aston University where he was International Gillette Research Fellow until 1974. From 1974 to 1982 he held appointments at Imperial College, London, in the Physiological Flow Studies Unit, the Department of Chemical Engineering and the Department of Pure and Applied Biology. He has published scientific papers in electrochemistry, biophysics, metallurgy, physiology and photosynthesis. Recently he set up Davis Rubin Associates Ltd, a joint publishing and research and development company.

Philip Webber is a research scientist in the Department of Physics at the Imperial College of Science and Technology. He gained his BSc in physics at Queen Elizabeth College, London, in 1973 and his PhD at Imperial College in 1977. After a short spell working for a computer software house he undertook post-doctoral research jointly in both the Chemical Engineering and Physics Departments at Imperial College. His special area of research is surface science and in particular the study of atomic and molecular interactions on metal surfaces. His publications include scientific papers in this field and articles on the effects of nuclear war. Dr Webber is a Member of the Institute of Physics.

Graeme Wilkinson is a Senior Lecturer in Computer Science at Kingston Polytechnic. He gained a first class honours degree in physics at Imperial College, London, in 1976 and a DPhil in atmospheric physics at the Clarendon Laboratory, Oxford University, in 1980. After working as a computer systems consultant he undertook post-doctoral research in computational physics at Queen Elizabeth College, University of London, and in satellite meteorology at the University of Reading. His publications include papers on atmospheric physics, satellite remote sensing and computational physics, as well as articles on the effects of nuclear weapons and satellite verification of arms control. Dr Wilkinson is a Fellow of the Royal Meteorological Society and a Member of the Institute of Physics.

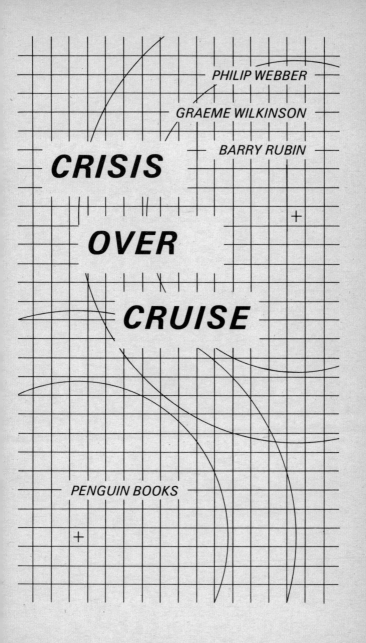

PHILIP WEBBER

GRAEME WILKINSON

BARRY RUBIN

# CRISIS

# OVER

# CRUISE

PENGUIN BOOKS

Penguin Books Ltd, Harmondsworth, Middlesex, England
Penguin Books, 40 West 23rd Street, New York, New York 10010, U.S.A.
Penguin Books Australia Ltd, Ringwood, Victoria, Australia
Penguin Books Canada Ltd, 2801 John Street, Markham, Ontario, Canada L3R 1B4
Penguin Books (N.Z.) Ltd, 182–190 Wairau Road, Auckland 10, New Zealand

First published 1983

Copyright © P. Webber, G. Wilkinson and B. Rubin, 1983
All rights reserved

Made and printed in Great Britain by
Cox and Wyman Ltd, Reading
Filmset in Monophoto Photina by Northumberland Press Ltd, Gateshead, Tyne and Wear

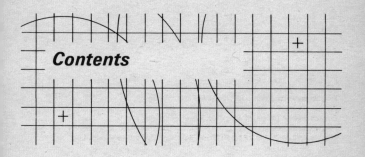

# Contents

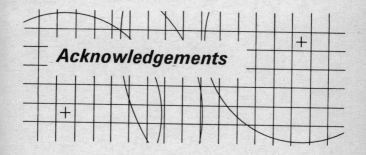

# *Acknowledgements*

We decided to write this book as a result of discussions with many people of differing viewpoints who, while they shared our concern over the nuclear arms race, did not feel that they knew enough to do anything about it. This book could not have been written without their inspiration and that of many close friends and colleagues who have supported us in this venture. In particular we are indebted to the following people for reading and commenting on the text: Dr Neil Turok, Dr David Caplin, Gail Daneker, Owen Greene, Dr Michael Barnett, Dr Michael Blackburn, Paul Wilkinson, Candice Temple and Jane Davis. We also want to thank all the staff of Penguin Books for preparing this book for press at such short notice and especially Rab MacWilliam for his commitment from the outset and Rachel Pyper for making the text readable and ensuring that we said what we meant to say and not something quite different. We also wish to thank our many colleagues in SANA (Scientists Against Nuclear Arms) for acting as sounding-boards for many of our ideas.

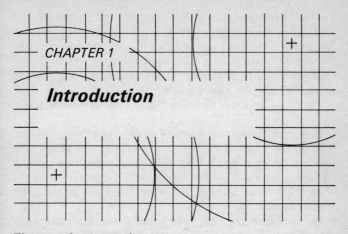

# CHAPTER 1

# Introduction

## The growing arsenals

Each year for the last thirty-eight years, the worldwide stockpile of nuclear weapons has been steadily increasing in size, diversity and sophistication, and no treaty has yet brought the arms race to a halt. Many politicians constantly reaffirm in public their desire for multilateral nuclear disarmament, but do little to support it in practice. The United Nations General Assembly Special Sessions on Disarmament (UNSSD 1 and UNSSD 2), held in 1978 and 1982, have achieved very little, primarily because the nuclear nations are only prepared to discuss disarmament from entrenched positions built on underlying mistrust. As a result, no real progress has been made.

With every new addition to the nuclear arsenals comes great danger; with each new type of weapon comes greater uncertainty. There are uncertainties over intentions, weapons capabilities, and over war fighting plans. These uncertainties decrease world security and make war more likely as each side indulges in contorted guessing games about the plans of the other. Further, as the number of weapons systems and strategies for their use multiply, so does the likelihood of nuclear war whether brought about by accident or design.

Some things are certain however. There will be no winners in a nuclear war. There is no effective means of civil defence against nuclear attack, despite some government claims to the contrary –

this has certainly been proved in recent studies by scientists[1] and members of the medical profession, including the British Medical Association.[2] Nuclear war would, at least for the northern hemisphere, be the greatest catastrophe of all time. As Khrushchev once pointed out, 'The ashes of Communism and the ashes of Capitalism will be indistinguishable.'[3]

The following facts in particular give cause for serious concern:

1. The current world nuclear arsenal stands at over 50,000 nuclear warheads with explosive powers ranging from about one hundredth of to over a thousand times the destructive power of the bomb which levelled Hiroshima. Yet only a few hundred warheads could destroy most of the major towns and cities in the northern hemisphere.

2. The total strength of the present nuclear arsenals is equivalent to about *one million* times the power of the Hiroshima bomb or some thirteen thousand million tons of TNT. Such destructive power is ten to a hundred times greater than that necessary to ensure the destruction of both East and West. It is, staggeringly, the equivalent of over *three tons* of high explosive for every man, woman and child on the earth.[4]

3. Nuclear weapons are spreading to more and more countries. Besides the USA and the USSR, Britain, France, China, and India have nuclear weapons. It is thought that South Africa has conducted a nuclear test in the South Atlantic. Countries such as Israel and Pakistan could soon build nuclear weapons or may have already done so.

4. As often as three times in less than a year armed nuclear bombers have prepared for take-off, and missile crews have begun preliminary launch procedures in response to a false red alert generated by computer malfunction.[5]

5. Over half the money allocated to the world's research scientists is spent on military or associated projects, while the developing countries spend five times as much foreign exchange on arms imports as on agricultural machinery.[6]

6. The total world military expenditure in 1982 amounted to over $650,000,000,000.[7] This sheer volume of military expenditure threatens to destabilize the international economic system, further raising the level of world tension.[8]

## New weapons

Despite these insane levels of destructive power and the severe drain on the world economy, the arms race has not even slowed down – quite the reverse, in fact. It is now entering a new phase with the development and production of large numbers of highly accurate 'counterforce' nuclear missiles of which Cruise and Pershing II are notable examples. NATO has decided to base these missiles in Europe from the end of 1983 onwards. They constitute the latest addition to the tip of a massive iceberg which, for the most part, remains hidden from direct view. The ground-launched cruise missiles (GLCMs) – 160 of which are destined for Britain – have acted as a major focus for debate precisely because they are so visible. They will roam the countryside on transporter lorries in time of tension (and on three-monthly practice runs) – they would not be hidden from view in submarines under the ocean, or in silos in remote areas on the plains of North America or on the steppes of central Asia.

The cruise missile, by virtue of its proximity to ordinary people, has been the focus of a re-emergent peace movement in which public awareness of the whole nuclear issue has become heightened. Scarcely a day goes by without mention of this issue in the media. Yet many people are still unaware of the speed and the implications of the new weapons developments. This, coupled with substantial propaganda by the superpowers and the British government, has for years resulted in widespread tacit approval for more and more weapons of mass destruction at great expense. Even now, when the majority of people are opposed to cruise missiles,[9] they often feel ill-equipped or too ill-informed to take any action about the impending disaster they so rightly fear. It has therefore been our aim to supply clear information about the characteristics of the new weapons and to assess their effect on our collective security. We have also attempted to examine the cause of our current nuclear dilemma and to suggest some possible positive steps towards a secure future for us all.

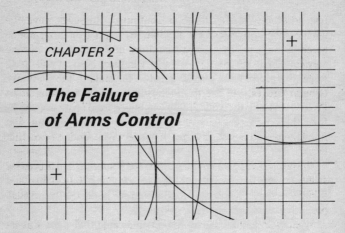

# CHAPTER 2

# *The Failure of Arms Control*

## The arms race

In early August 1945, the nuclear age was rudely ushered in, as nuclear bombs were exploded in the skies above Hiroshima and Nagasaki, causing sudden destruction and loss of life of a magnitude hitherto unseen in war. Several hundreds of thousands of people were killed. Many more were injured or maimed for life. Some are still dying today.[1]

That the nuclear bomb was developed was a direct consequence of 'advances' in scientific knowledge. Scientists first observed the reaction now known as nuclear fission in 1938.[2] High energy particles hitting the nucleus of an atom were observed to cause it to break up into smaller pieces which in turn gave off very energetic particles (radiation).

By 1939, at the outbreak of World War II, several scientists had realized that a very powerful bomb might possibly be made by starting off a nuclear chain reaction, as more and more atoms were split and they in turn split others. In October, Albert Einstein wrote to the US President, Roosevelt, warning him of the possible danger that the Germans might be the first to develop such an atomic bomb.

By 1942, Enrico Fermi had demonstrated the first nuclear chain reaction at Chicago University. An atomic bomb was now a very real possibility and as the war continued, Roosevelt gave the go-ahead for the highly secret 'Manhattan Project' to build an atomic bomb in the new Los Alamos laboratory in a remote part of New Mexico. There is some doubt as to whether, even at this early stage, the project was purely aimed at forestalling the Germans. General Groves, the overall military director of the Manhattan Project, was later to testify: 'There was never, from about two weeks from the time I took charge, any illusion on my part but that Russia was our enemy, and that the project was conducted on that basis.'[3]

The project was given almost unlimited resources and proceeded swiftly, it 'was accomplished ... by an army of 120,000 men and a budget equal to half the normal annual budget of the British people for the whole of their government'.[4]

By early 1945, intelligence reports indicated that there was no threat from a German atomic bomb. Consequently, some of the scientists in the bomb team did not feel that the project was still justified and one decided to leave. Nevertheless, on 16 July the first atomic bomb was exploded in a test at Alamogordo in the New Mexico desert. All who witnessed the test were profoundly affected. Dr Oppenheimer, the scientific director of the project, was moved to quote, from the *Bhagavad-Gita*, the Hindu Song of God: 'If the radiance of a thousand suns were to burst at once into the sky that would be like the splendour of the Mighty One ... I am become Death, the shatterer of worlds.' A report sent to the new President of the USA, Harry S. Truman, who was attending a meeting with Stalin and Churchill at Potsdam, stated: 'It lighted every peak, crevasse and ridge of the nearby mountain range with a clarity and beauty that cannot be described but must be seen to be imagined. It was the beauty the great poets dream about.'[5]

Three weeks later atomic bombs were used with devastating effect on human populations. The total annihilation of Hiroshima and Nagasaki vividly demonstrated the power of nuclear weapons and led Stalin, within two weeks, to issue the following order to Academician Kurchatov, in charge of the Russian atomic bomb project: 'A single demand of you, comrades: provide us with atomic weapons in the shortest possible time. You know that Hiroshima

## Hiroshima and Nagasaki

H. L. Stimson, American Secretary of War 1940–45, chaired the so-called Interim Committee to advise the American president about the development of the atomic bomb. In its minutes of 31 May 1945, the Interim Committee noted that: 'the most desirable target would be a vital war plant employing a large number of workers and *closely surrounded by workers houses*'* (our italics).

On 1 June 1945, after its discussions with the Scientific Panel, the Committee unanimously adopted the following recommendations:†

1. The bomb should be used against Japan as soon as possible.
2. It should be used on a dual target – that is, a military installation or war plant surrounded by, or adjacent to, houses and other buildings most susceptible to damage.
3. It should be used without prior warning [of the nature of the weapon].

One member of the committee later changed his view and dissented from recommendation 3.

By 25 July 1945, four targets in Japan had been chosen:§ Hiroshima, Kokura, Niigata and Nagasaki. Hiroshima was selected for the first bomb. It had previously been spared conventional bombing – the effects of the new atomic weapon would thus be clearly seen. The second target chosen was Niigata but on 9 August the weather over this city was cloudy and the bomber flew on to Nagasaki.

In each attack several B-29 Stratofortress bombers flew in; one dropped the bomb, while the others remained distant from the explosion, carried observers and dropped scientific measuring instruments. The two weapons dropped – 'Little Boy' and 'Fat Man' – were of different construction; made with uranium-235 and plutonium-239 respectively, to see if both methods of construction would work.

* Notes of the Interim Committee Meeting 31 May 1945, Manhattan Engineering District Papers, National Archives, Washington D.C.

† H. L. Stimson, 'The Decision to Use the Atomic Bomb', *Harpers Magazine*, February 1947 (pp. 97–107).

§ Declassified memo from General T. T. Handy, Acting Chief of Staff, War Department, to General C. Spaats, Commanding General, U S Army Strategic Air Forces, 25 July 1945.

has shaken the world. The equilibrium has been destroyed ... Provide the bomb – it will remove a great danger from us.'[6] And so the arms race began.

By 1949, the USSR too had an atomic bomb. By the early 1950s, both the USSR and the USA had developed the H-bomb, a much more powerful weapon than the atomic bomb with virtually no upper limit to its explosive power.

Since then, the arms race has continued unchecked through three major stages. First, in the early 1950s, the USA deployed 300 nuclear-armed propeller-driven B-29 and B-50 bombers. The USSR followed suit by the mid-fifties, deploying 300 Tu-4 bombers (a copy of the B-29). By 1960, the USA had deployed over 2000 B-52 and B-47 jet bombers, while the USSR had deployed only 150 Tu-95 and Mya-4 propeller-driven bombers.

The second stage followed with the development of intercontinental ballistic missiles (ICBMs) and submarine-launched ballistic missiles (SLBMs). By the late sixties, both sides had deployed over one thousand of these missiles. The USA progressively phased out a fraction of their bomber force as the new missiles were introduced.

Stage three, throughout the seventies (see Figure 1), saw a sharp escalation in the arms race with the development of more than one warhead per missile-launcher. As a result, the total number of warheads trebled, despite two major sets of arms limitation talks.

Throughout this period since the Second World War, the number of weapons in the US arsenal has exceeded the number in the Soviet arsenal. Moreover, the USA has led the arms race by initiating all the new technological innovations. It is generally accepted that the USA has a five- to ten-year technological lead over the USSR – the USA introduced multiple warheads in 1970, five years ahead of the USSR, for example.

The arms race is now entering a fourth stage, led again by the USA, with the development of highly accurate 'counterforce' missiles such as Cruise. By the 1990s, the arms race may move into a fifth phase with the development and deployment of space-borne laser- and particle-beam weapons (see Appendix 2).

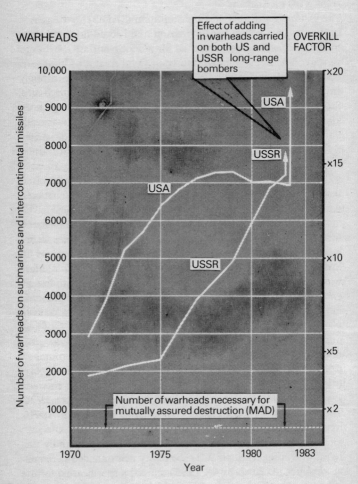

*Figure 1.* The arms race
(Data from notes 7, 8, 9,)

## Arms limitation treaties

The first talks on strategic arms limitation (SALT-1) were started in the late 1960s by Lyndon Johnson and Leonid Brezhnev. The treaty was eventually signed in May 1972 during the Nixon administration and came into force in October. It was, however, little more than a public charade, as both sides were actively engaged in new weapons developments which evaded the treaty. Since SALT-1 the total numbers of missile-launchers have been kept at roughly the agreed levels, but the numbers of warheads have risen dramatically – both East and West have developed more compact warheads, enabling one launcher to carry many independently targetable warheads (known as MIRVing, Multiple Independently-targetable Re-entry Vehicles). In terms of destruction it is the number of warheads, not the number of launchers, which counts. The constraint on anti-ballistic missile (ABM) defences has been largely irrelevant because neither side has been able to develop an effective system. The defensive missiles themselves carry nuclear warheads which, once detonated, cause an intense pulse of electromagnetic radiation which would interfere with the guidance system of all the others. Also they can destroy each other by heat and radiation (known as fratricide). The only anti-ballistic missile system in existence is the Russian 'Galosh' system of thirty-two missiles (recently reduced from sixty-four missiles) which rings Moscow.

After the SALT-1 treaty came into force, a new round of negotiations was begun, which culminated in the SALT-2 treaty, the basis of which was outlined in a summit meeting between Presidents Ford and Brezhnev in Vladivostok in November 1974. The main treaty itself was eventually signed in June 1979 after much deliberation from both sides. It is unlikely to come into force, however, because the US Senate has yet to ratify the treaty and probably never will. The treaty was intended to remain in force until December 1985 and included a specification for the reduction in the total number of strategic missiles from an initial figure of 2400 to a figure of 2250 by the end of 1981. It would, however, have had a small impact on the total number of missiles because the permitted total of 2400, while slightly fewer than the Soviet arsenal, was larger than the US arsenal. Also, and rather more importantly, the treaty would not have made much impact on the total number of nuclear warheads, in which the USA has always exceeded the USSR. Nevertheless, in some respects the SALT-2 treaty went considerably further than SALT-1 in that it included long-range bombers in the reckoning and also prohibited the production of more than one new type of ICBM.

Despite its limitations, SALT-2 would at least have represented some attempt at arms limitation and should have been ratified by the US Senate. Indeed, Secretary Harold Brown in the US Department of Defense Report for 1980 said: 'We are nearing the completion of a SALT-2 agreement that will contribute to the security of the United States and its allies ... The SALT agreement that is nearing completion will permit us to maintain the nuclear balance at lower levels with fewer launchers than the Soviets could deploy without agreement. Avoiding the necessity to match such growth in the Soviet forces will leave US (and Soviet) resources free for other needs and avoid the political costs of unrestrained competition.'[10] In fact, the treaty has not even been offered to the Senate for their decision but was withdrawn by President Carter in protest at the Soviet invasion of Afghanistan.

President Reagan has shelved SALT-2 in favour of his own treaty to *reduce*, not limit, nuclear weapons – a proposal of which he is somewhat proud. The strategic arms reduction treaty (START) which Reagan has proposed would, in fact, create far greater imbalance between East and West than SALT-2. In his scheme, Reagan has opted for a one-third reduction in the number of warheads of strategic ballistic missiles. This plan is unrealistic as it takes no account of the large number of air- and sea-launched cruise missiles which the USA has started to deploy on its bombers and plans to deploy on submarines and ships. Also, the plan would not prevent the production of new missiles (e.g. MX and Trident D-5) with sufficiently high accuracy to hit missile silos which could be used to replace existing missiles. The net effect of the Reagan START proposal is shown in Figure 2. If implemented according to Reagan's plans, START will result in a net *increase* in the number of US strategic warheads by the year

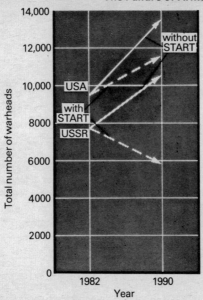

*Figure 2.* The START proposals
(Data from notes 8, 9)

1990, as a result of the massive planned deployment of several thousand cruise missiles, whilst causing a *reduction* in the Soviet arsenal. START would thus actually widen the gap between the US and Soviet forces and clearly cannot be taken seriously by the USSR as it stands. With proposals as unrealistic as START on the negotiating table, the prospects for arms control by negotiation seem as remote now as they have for the last thirty-eight years.

## The SALT-1 treaty

In force October 1972, this treaty placed a five-year freeze on the numbers of missile-launchers as follows:

USA      1000 ICBMs and 710 SLBMs
USSR    1408 ICBMs and 950 SLBMs

The Soviet Union was allowed more missiles to compensate for the large numbers of US B-52 long-range bombers. Anti-ballistic missile (ABM) systems were limited to two areas in each country: one to defend the national capital and one to defend an ICBM missile silo complex. In 1976 ABM systems were limited to just one site in each country.

## The SALT-2 treaty

The principal components of the treaty were the following:

(i) a limit of 2400 strategic delivery vehicles for both sides (including ICBM and SLBM launchers, air-to-surface ballistic missiles (ASBMs) with a range of more than 600 kilometres, and, for the first time, long-range bombers).

(ii) a subsidiary limit of 1320 on the number of delivery vehicles equipped with MIRVs (this category included bombers carrying cruise missiles with ranges greater than 600 kilometres). This subsidiary limit is also subject to the following restrictions: that the total number of MIRVed ICBMs, SLBMs and ASBMs should not exceed 1200 and that the total number of MIRVed ICBMs should not exceed 820.

(iii) a freeze on the number of warheads on each existing MIRVed ICBM.

(iv) a ban on testing and deploying new types of ICBM except for one which may carry no more than ten warheads per launcher.

## The Phases of the Arms Race

| | |
|---|---|
| 1. The rise of long-range bomber forces | 1950–61 |
| 2. Extensive deployment of I C B Ms and S L B Ms | 1962–73 |
| 3. Deployment of multiple warheads (M I R Vs) | 1970–79 |
| 4. Deployment of highly accurate 'counterforce' weapons | 1983–90? |
| 5. Space-borne laser- and particle-beam weapons? | 1990–2000? |

# CHAPTER 3

# Cruise and
# the New Weapons

## Early cruise missiles

The basic concept of the cruise missile is very old and dates back to the Second World War. The first cruise missiles were the German V-1 'doodlebugs', which were used to attack London in 1944. They were fired from launching strips in northern France and Belgium, had a range of about 100 miles and carried a high explosive (non-nuclear) warhead. They had the advantage that they could be sent over in broad daylight when it was too dangerous for manned bombers. They could have had a serious effect on the outcome of the war had it not been for the early destruction of their launch sites.

Since the war, various types of cruise missile have been produced by the superpowers to carry both nuclear and conventional warheads, designed for launch from air, ground and sea.

Between 1954 and 1964, 'Regulus' submarine-launched cruise missiles with a range of about 350 miles were in service with the US Navy. These missiles were 'dual-capable' – that is, they could carry either conventional or nuclear warheads. The USSR produced similar SS-N-3 'Shaddock' (the NATO code-name) sea-launched cruise missiles which were based on submarines and cruisers. The US Air Force also had ground-launched 'Matador' cruise missiles in Germany in the mid-1950s with a range of about 500 miles. These were replaced by 'Mace' A and B missiles in the early 1960s with ranges of about 1000 miles. They were put in silos 'hardened' against blast, but were eventually removed on account of their vulnerability to air attack. From 1961, the United States put 'Hound Dog' air-to-surface cruise missiles on its long-range bomber force. These missiles had nuclear warheads with explosive yields in the kiloton range (one kT is equivalent in explosive power to 1000 tons of TNT) and they could fly for about 500 miles. The USSR deployed similar air-launched weapons such as the AS-3 'Kangaroo' and AS-4 'Kitchen' missiles with ranges of about 300–400 miles. These early air-launched cruise missiles were designed to increase the effectiveness of bombers because the missiles could be fired off at a safe distance from anti-aircraft defences.

## The modern cruise missile

All the older generation cruise missiles had significant limitations, principally very poor accuracy and short range (less than 1000 miles or so). The only cruise missile of intercontinental range which was developed – the 'Snark' – was a complete fiasco: 'The average miss distance was over 1000 miles. At least one came down in the wrong hemisphere, disappearing somewhere in the interior of Brazil.'[1] The early missiles could also carry only relatively small warheads and could not be used as long-range strategic weapons in their own right. By the early 1970s, however, US scientists and engineers had made several significant technological advances. These were the development of highly accurate missile-navigation techniques, extremely powerful but light nuclear warheads and small but highly efficient jet engines. These innovations completely revolutionized the concept of the 'cruise missile' and opened up the possibility of comparatively inexpensive long-range, high-accuracy cruise missiles with high yield warheads – weapons of major strategic importance. This new generation of cruise missiles has now been under production for several years and the first missiles have already been placed on B-52 bombers.[2] The Soviet Union remains well behind in this technology.

The new cruise missiles have been developed by two US companies under contract to the US Department of Defense. Two

## Some Facts on Cruise Missiles

Cruise missiles are small, low-flying, pilotless, jet-propelled planes, which can carry either a 200 kT nuclear warhead (equivalent to 16 Hiroshimas) or a 1000 lb. high explosive conventional bomb.

Cruise missiles are designed to fly entirely within the earth's atmosphere unlike ballistic missiles, which are launched into space before re-entering the atmosphere to fall on to their targets.

Because they are small and fly low (at 50–300 feet) they are very difficult to detect on radar.

Flying at 550 m.p.h., cruise missiles would take two to three hours to reach their targets.

Using maps stored in a miniature computer on board, they achieve very high accuracy, and can arrive within fifty yards of a target after a 1500 mile flight.

There are several kinds of cruise missile in production – air-launched, sea-launched, and ground-launched (GLCM). It is the GLCMs that are due to be based at Greenham Common and Molesworth.

In times of crisis they will be moved from their bases on 40-ton lorries in large convoys escorted by dozens of armed security guards and support services. They will certainly not 'melt into the countryside', as the Government claims.

principal makes of cruise missile are now being produced: these are the AGM-86B built by Boeing Corporation (better known for its jet airliners) and the 'Tomahawk' cruise missile (of which there are several versions) built by the General Dynamics Corporation. The US government has decided to install these missiles on aircraft, surface ships, submarines and ground-launchers. The Boeing AGM-86B was selected as the new air-launched cruise missile in a fly-off between ten Tomahawks and ten AGM-86Bs. In this trial four of the Tomahawks crashed compared with only three AGM-86Bs (although a further one went off course). To avoid too much disappointment to General Dynamics, however, a week after the contract was awarded to Boeing, General Dynamics were awarded a contract to produce a new medium-range air-to-surface cruise missile (MRASM).[3]

There are three types of sea-launched cruise missile: those designed for attacking land targets with either nuclear or conventional warheads (called the TLAM-N and TLAM-C) and one for attacking sea targets with a conventional warhead (TASM).

The procurement of the new generation of cruise missiles represents the most substantial escalation in the arms race since the advent of multiple warheads on ballistic missiles in the 1970s. A total of 464 ground-launched cruise missiles are due to be based in Europe by 1988 (beginning December 1983) at a total cost of $3,950,000,000.[4] A total of 560 have recently been ordered.[5] The US government originally ordered a total of 3780 air-launched cruise missiles for its B-52 and forthcoming B-1 bombers and 3994 cruise missiles for sea launch.[6] These figures have now been reduced to about 1500 on account of improvements in Soviet air defences and because the new 'stealth cruise' is under development. This will be made virtually invisible to radar and infra-red sensors by using materials with low radar reflectivity (such as carbon fibre) and engines with cooled exhausts.

All versions of the new cruise missile have roughly the same characteristics and are all built to approximately the same design (see Figure 3). They are about 20 feet long, 2 feet in diameter and weigh about 1½ tons. They are powered by the Williams Research light turbofan engine, weighing only 150 lb., which can develop a thrust up to 600 lb.[7] The sea- and ground-launch versions are fired out of tubes on ships, submarines or transporter lorries

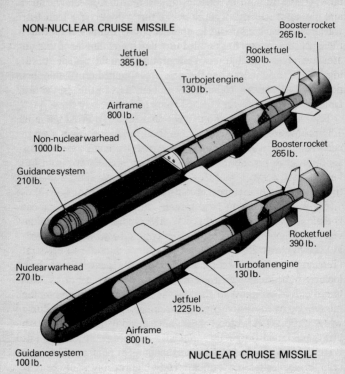

NON-NUCLEAR CRUISE MISSILE

Booster rocket
265 lb.

Rocket fuel
390 lb.

Jet fuel
385 lb.

Turbojet engine
130 lb.

Airframe
800 lb.

Non-nuclear warhead
1000 lb.

Booster rocket
265 lb.

Guidance system
210 lb.

Nuclear warhead
270 lb.

Rocket fuel
390 lb.

Turbofan engine
130 lb.

Jet fuel
1225 lb.

Airframe
800 lb.

Guidance system
100 lb.

NUCLEAR CRUISE MISSILE

*Figure 3.* The basic design of the Tomahawk cruise missile
Both the nuclear and non-nuclear cruise missiles are 21 inches in diameter and 20 feet long and appear identical. The nuclear warhead, however, takes up less space than the conventional explosive, leaving more room for fuel and giving the nuclear cruise missile a longer range.

respectively. They carry booster rockets to launch themselves into the air. A few seconds after launch the booster is jettisoned and the jet engine takes over. The air-launched version does not require a booster, the missile is merely released from a pylon under an aircraft wing or alternatively out of a bomb bay. They can even be launched after some minor modifications from commercial airliners such as the DC-10 or Boeing-747.

Most of the internal space of the long-range cruise missile is taken up by the jet fuel, the remainder by the nuclear warhead and the guidance system. The yield of the W-80 or W-84 nuclear warhead can be set in a range up to 200 kT – this is sixteen times the explosive power of the Hiroshima bomb and can devastate an area two and a half times as wide; little would be left standing within two miles of ground-zero – the point immediately beneath the explosion (see Figure 4 for the effect of this on central London).

The tactical sea-launched cruise missiles (the TLAM-C and TASM) have a range of a few hundred miles and carry a large conventional explosive warhead. These non-nuclear cruise missiles simply cannot be distinguished by satellite surveillance from the longer-range nuclear cruise missiles, which substantially increases the difficulty of verifying arms control agreements.

The most sophisticated component of the new cruise missiles is their guidance system. A special computer system has been developed to enable them to hit their targets to within fifty yards at least fifty per cent of the time. This system, known as TERCOM (Terrain Contour Matching, see Appendix 1), uses downward-looking radar to build up a map of local ground features. This is compared with a map already stored in the computer as the missile flies along. In this way the missile should always know where it is and can therefore make corrections to its flight path if it is blown off course by the wind, for example. By doing this it can hit its target with great precision, even after a long 1500-mile flight at low level. The extremely high accuracy of the new cruise missiles is a new and significant development. This accuracy enables them to score practically direct hits on their chosen targets and to destroy enemy missiles even in hardened concrete silos.

The production of the cruise missiles has not been accomplished without its problems. The TERCOM guidance system in particular has presented several technical difficulties. The snow-covered Arctic, for example, provides few ground features for an airborne cruise to recognize. Canada intends to help solve this particular problem by allowing missile tests at the Cold Lake weapons range in Alberta. This is a remote area which is representative of Arctic

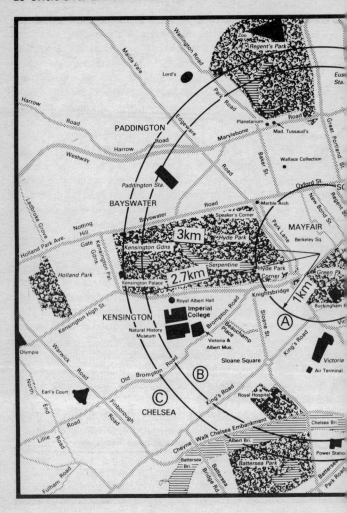

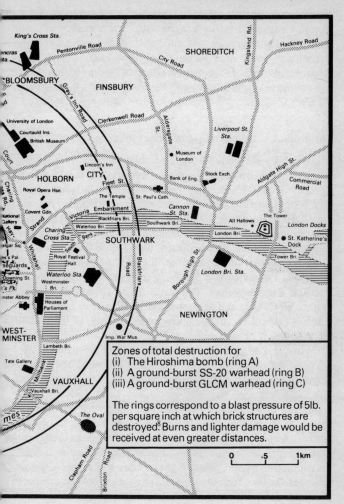

Zones of total destruction for
(i)   The Hiroshima bomb (ring A)
(ii)  A ground-burst SS-20 warhead (ring B)
(iii) A ground-burst GLCM warhead (ring C)

The rings correspond to a blast pressure of 5lb. per square inch at which brick structures are destroyed. Burns and lighter damage would be received at even greater distances.

0        .5        1km

terrain, and which is similar to much of the Soviet Union.[9] Although Canada is a non-nuclear nation, it is part of NATO and its involvement actually goes further than the test programme. A company based near Toronto has been building part of the guidance systems – Litton Systems Canada Ltd has been awarded two contracts worth $80,000,000 in total by the US Department of Defense.[10]

## The ground-launched cruise missiles for Europe

In December 1979, NATO took the decision to 'modernize' its long-range European strategic weapons – known also as the 'theatre' nuclear forces. This decision called for the installation of 464 GLCMs in western Europe (together with a large number of Pershing II intermediate-range ballistic missiles) by 1988; the first of them to be deployed in 1983. In June 1980, the British Defence Secretary, Francis Pym, announced that 160 of the 464 GLCMs would be based in England at the US Air Force bases at Greenham Common near Newbury in Berkshire, and at Molesworth in Cambridgeshire. The plans are for Greenham Common to have 96 GLCMs and be operational by the end of 1983. Molesworth is to have 64 and be operational by 1988. Of the remaining missiles, 112 are designated for Comiso in Sicily, 96 for Germany, and 48 each for Belgium and the Netherlands.

The GLCMs are launched from mobile lorries called 'Transporter-Erector-Launchers' (TELs), each of which has four missile tubes. The TELs, although stationed at military bases, will actually be driven out into the countryside in times of perceived tension or threat. At their home base the TELs will be housed in concrete bunkers which will protect them from air attack (although not from a direct nuclear hit). On dispersal the TELs move out into the country in 'flights'.[11] Each flight (or convoy) consists of twenty-two vehicles (see Figure 5) – four TELs, two heavily armoured Launch Control Centres (LCCs), plus sixteen support vehicles. Each TEL is 55 feet long and weighs 35 tons. The LCCs are 57 feet long and also weigh 35 tons – the convoys will hardly be unobtrusive. Each convoy will contain sixty-nine personnel, most of whom will be security guards. Greenham Common is to house six of these convoys and Molesworth four. The missiles will be

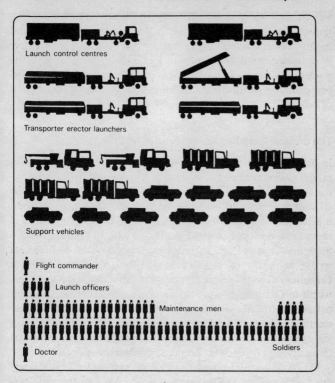

*Figure 5.* The supporting cast for cruise
Reproduced by kind permission of the New Scientist

launched entirely by US personnel. The launch crew are protected inside the LCC against biological and chemical attack. They would launch the missiles by typing a six digit code number into a computer keyboard. The code would be relayed by satellite from the US European Command (EUCOM) near Stuttgart in Germany, which has direct links with the White House.[12]

Once on the move the convoys will have the freedom of the roads and indeed could ford streams more than a metre deep and climb hills. Very little, short of a well-armed military force, would be able to stop them. In principle the British government expects

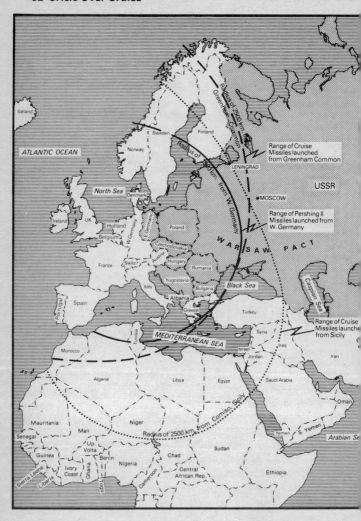

*Figure 6.*

— — — Range of cruise missiles launched from Greenham Common

............... Range of cruise missiles launched from Comiso, Sicily

———— Range of Pershing II launched from West Germany

to be 'consulted' before the GLCMs are ever used, although this gives no power of veto over their firing.

Due to their relatively limited range, the choice of home bases for the European GLCMs in the UK and Sicily is somewhat inappropriate. If they are intended for use against the USSR they should all be based in Germany, from where they can strike deep into Soviet territory. According to present plans, however, Britain is to get the lion's share. Figure 6 shows their approximate range if based in southern England and in Sicily. It is apparent that, given a range of about 1500 miles, they can barely reach Moscow from these two locations. It has also been pointed out that Sicily is a most unlikely location for GLCMs aimed at Russia.[13] It is, however, an ideal position from which to attack Libya, together with much of North Africa and the Middle East.

## Pershing II

The second component of the NATO theatre nuclear modernization is the proposed installation of new Pershing II intermediate-range ballistic missiles in Europe. They are intended to replace the 400-mile-range Pershing I missiles deployed since 1962 in Germany. The Pershing II is, however, a vastly more threatening weapon than the Pershing I.

The initial research and development phase of the Pershing II project began in 1974. The final 1978 design specification was for a fast, highly accurate ballistic missile with a range of about 1100 miles. In early 1979, the Martin-Marietta corporation was awarded a full development contract by the US Department of Defense.

The Pershing II (see Figure 7) is a 33 feet long, 7 ton, two stage solid-fuelled rocket, which has the most accurate navigation system of any ballistic missile so far produced. The nose-cone of the Pershing II is equipped with the new RADAG (radar area guidance) system made by the Goodyear Corporation (see Appendix 1), which scans the target area with a radar beam as the warhead falls towards the ground in the terminal stages of its short space-flight. This system, not conceptually unlike the cruise TERCOM system, enables the missiles to home in to within forty yards of

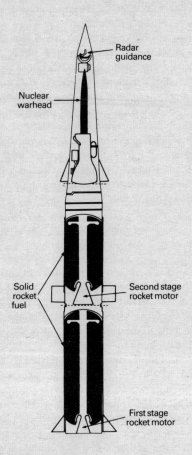

*Figure 7*. The Pershing II missile

their designated targets at least fifty per cent of the time. This accuracy is far greater than that needed for a deterrent force. This raises questions about the purpose of these new missiles in Europe and the thinking behind the lengthy RADAG development. As with Cruise, this high accuracy enables them to destroy enemy missiles in their silos.

According to NATO's publicized plan, a total of 108 Pershing IIs are to be based in West Germany from 1983 to replace the same number of Pershing Is. Early in 1983, however, it emerged that the Pentagon had ordered a total of 311 Pershing IIs.[5] It is not uncommon for a few extra missiles to be ordered for test firings, etc., but over-ordering by a factor of three is unprecedented. This has given rise to speculation that the planned 108 launchers can actually be reloaded with fresh missiles after the first ones have been fired.

The missiles are to be based in the south-western part of Germany and will be organized in three battalions of thirty-six mobile launchers.[14] Every group of three launchers is controlled by a separate firing platoon which can in practice launch three missiles simultaneously. The rockets travel at over 5000 m.p.h. and could reach parts of the western Soviet Union in under ten minutes. They could get to targets in Eastern Europe within three to four minutes. Figure 6 shows the approximate range for the Pershing IIs based in Germany. The Pershing IIs are to be equipped with the W-85 selectable yield warhead. These warheads are believed to be capable of giving a yield of 250 kT (twenty times the power of the Hiroshima bomb) but may in practice be selected to give a comparatively modest 10 kT yield – roughly the same as Hiroshima. Even this 'modest' yield can destroy an area two miles in diameter. In addition, earth-penetrating warheads have been developed. A 5 kT earth-penetrating weapon produces as powerful an underground shock as a 100 kT weapon exploded at the surface. This warhead is clearly designed to destroy underground command bunkers or missiles in their silos.

Like Cruise, the development of the Pershing II missiles has not been accomplished without some major setbacks. Several of the early test firings failed dismally. In a test conducted in July 1982, a Pershing II exploded seventeen seconds after launch.[15] In November 1982, a Pershing II managed to complete a 100-mile test flight but the RADAG system failed to work correctly. A completely successful test was not performed until January 1983. The US Congress voted funds for the production of only twenty-one Pershing IIs in 1982 due to its poor test performance record. The funding is now being raised to enable the full production programme to be completed at an estimated overall cost of $2,800,000,000.[16]

## The SS-20 missile

These missiles are essentially the final two stages of the SS-16 mobile intercontinental missile which was never deployed.

In 1976 the Soviet Union began to set up its first SS-20 intermediate-range ballistic missiles which were first flight-tested in 1974. Since then they have been produced roughly at the rate of one per week and by 1983 there were believed to be a total of 333 SS-20s in existence on Soviet territory. The existence of these weapons has been used by NATO as the justification for the deployment of the cruise and Pershing II missiles.

Technologically, the SS-20 is equivalent to the *previous* generation of American missiles (with about the same accuracy as the old US Minuteman II, first deployed in 1966), but it is nevertheless one of the most advanced missiles in the Soviet arsenal. The SS-20s are mobile missiles launched from heavy transporter vehicles (see Figure 8) – rather like GLCMs. They are over 50 feet long, somewhat larger than the Pershing II. Each SS-20 missile carries three 150 kT warheads which can be directed at separate targets. Each warhead has twelve times the explosive power of the Hiroshima bomb and would devastate an area nearly four miles across and cause serious injury and burns at a range of 3–4 miles from ground-zero. One SS-20 warhead could destroy the heart of London (see Figure 4). The SS-20s are currently based at eight locations in western Russia, near the Ural Mountains, and in the far eastern side of the continent. It is estimated that about two thirds of them are targeted on western Europe, the rest on China. With a range of 2750 miles, any SS-20s based to the west of the Urals could strike at any part of western Europe, including the UK. The SS-20s are under the control of the Soviet Strategic Rocket Forces, which recruit only the brightest military officers known as the 'soldier intellectuals'.[17] In time of crisis the SS-20s would be dispersed to pre-planned launching positions.

The Soviet justification for the production of the SS-20 is twofold, based partly on the nature of the perceived traditional threat to the Soviet homeland, and partly on the technological necessity of replacing old, vulnerable and inferior missiles.

The older medium-range missiles (the SS-4s and the SS-5s) are

*Figure 8.* The firing of the Russian SS-20 missile from its mobile launcher

now too vulnerable to attack. These old missiles, first deployed in 1959 and 1961 respectively, rely on unstable liquid fuel, which must be pumped into the rockets, taking up to an hour, before they can be launched. They also have very low accuracy (half a mile to a mile). Eighty per cent of them are based above ground and not in protective silos. The mobile SS-20s which burn solid fuel can, however, be launched at very short notice and also have a much improved accuracy of about 400 yards – but this does not nearly match the capability of the American TERCOM and RADAG guidance systems.

## The new ICBMs: the MX and the SS-18

Along with the recent increases in the accuracy of missiles there has been a growing fear, in both the USA and the USSR, for the safety of their ICBM forces against surprise attack. The United States has initiated development of a new intercontinental missile called MX (for 'Missile Experimental' – President Reagan has chosen to rename this missile as 'Peace-keeper'). The driving force behind the MX development is supposedly to provide an ICBM force invulnerable to any Soviet nuclear attack. In order to try and achieve this invulnerability, no less than *thirty-three* bizarre missile-siting schemes have been proposed to date. 'They either threaten the country with bankruptcy, breach one or more international treaties, are based on improbable (not to say Heath Robinson type) technical theories, or fail to achieve the invulnerability for which the system was originally proposed.'[18]

One plan is the Wyoming 'dense-pack' scheme. In this scheme, the MX missiles would be based in silos in close proximity to each other – the theory being that the first incoming Soviet missiles would destroy a few MXs but also create such a huge cloud of radioactive debris over the silo site that subsequent missiles would be prevented from homing in accurately on their targets, thus ensuring the survivability of the rest of the force. In fact, any attacker could get round the problem by timing several warheads to explode simultaneously.

Another scheme, known as 'closed-loop', would involve the construction of 200 loop roads about thirty miles in circumference, along each of which there would be spur roads linking to twenty-three underground concrete shelters. The idea is that the missiles would be based on 300-ton mobile transporter launchers which could be driven around from shelter to shelter. The Russians would not know which shelters the launchers were hiding in, and would have to destroy all 4600 of them to be sure of destroying the complete MX force of 200 missiles (see Figure 9).

There have been other proposed schemes for MX, such as attaching them outside the hulls of a large number of submarines which would hide in US coastal waters, or alternatively putting them

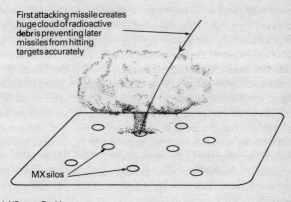

First attacking missile creates huge cloud of radioactive debris is preventing later missiles from hitting targets accurately

MX silos

(a) 'Dense-Pack'

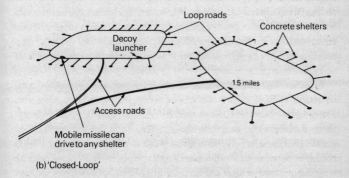

Loop roads

Decoy launcher

Concrete shelters

1.5 miles

Access roads

Mobile missile can drive to any shelter

(b) 'Closed-Loop'

*Figure 9.* Two deployment modes for the MX missile

in aircraft, from which they could be dropped by parachute before firing their rocket motors in mid-air.

So far no scheme has finally been accepted by the US Congress.

The Carter administration favoured closed-loop and the Reagan administration originally favoured dense-pack. But the theory behind dense-pack was 'greeted with derision' by Congress, and Reagan appointed a Presidential Commission to look into the MX problem.[19] Although President Reagan is intent on going ahead with the MX development there has been much opposition on the grounds of the cost – $35,000,000,000.[20]

The latest scheme is for a force of 100 MX missiles in super-hardened 'Minuteman III' silos, possibly backed up by 100 light-weight 'Midgetman' runabout missiles to wander randomly about Montana, Wyoming, Colorado and Utah.[21] This scheme will still cost about $14,000,000,000.

The MX missiles are planned to have ten warheads each, with a high accuracy of 100 yards or better, which means that they could be used to destroy Soviet missiles in their silos. If deployed, the MX missile system will represent a massive escalation of the arms race.

Part of the supposed justification for the deployment of the MX missile is the deployment of the Russian SS-18 missile. The public justification given by the military was that the SS-18s, some of which have a large warhead of ten to twenty megatons (MT) and an accuracy of about 400 yards, could knock out the US Minuteman ICBM force in a surprise attack. This justification never really held water because there are simply not enough SS-18 warheads of this size to destroy a sizeable proportion of the Minuteman force. Some SS-18s are fitted with multiple warheads of 500 kilotons, but these are insufficiently powerful, in combination with this accuracy, to have a good chance of knocking out the Minuteman silos. More recently, further evidence from the Massachusetts Institute of Technology, and from CIA-leaked documents, questions the accuracy claimed for the SS-18 missile. Observations of SS-18 and SS-19 test firings indicated that they 'wobbled' too much in flight to hit Minuteman missile silos.[22]

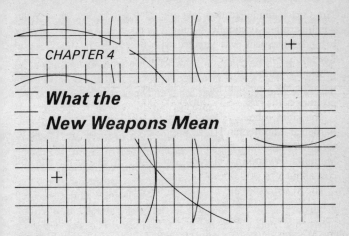

# CHAPTER 4

## What the New Weapons Mean

### Cruise

To some people the deployment of ground-launched cruise missiles in Europe is a much needed response to the might of the Soviet military machine. To others these missiles represent a totally unnecessary escalation in the arms race which endangers peace. These two views are fundamentally irreconcilable. The only way of deciding between them is to determine whether, on balance, cruise missiles increase or decrease our safety.

The main government argument in support of cruise missiles is that they are to be deployed to off-set the imbalance created by the Soviet deployment of several hundred SS-20 medium-range missiles.

The planned deployment of the SS-20 had been known to NATO since 1976.[1] It was, in fact, not a new missile, but the top two stages of the unsuccessful intercontinental-range SS-16 missile. In 1977 and 1978 no special response to the missile was sought by the NATO alliance. The 400 warheads attached to four Poseidon submarines under European NATO command, and 192 warheads on the UK Polaris submarines were regarded as adequate. In October 1977 German Chancellor Schmidt, in a speech to the International Institute of Strategic Studies in London, pointed out that any disparities in theatre nuclear forces would become more noticeable if both superpowers reduced their numbers of strategic weapons. By December 1979, however, it was strongly argued that the Cruise and Pershing II programme was needed to counter the threat from the SS-20, and NATO took its so-called 'dual track' decision to deploy these missiles while pressing for reductions in theatre nuclear forces. It seems, however, that the SS-20 missile was only brought into the argument once popular consent was being sought for the new missiles and that, in reality, it bears little relation to the real reasons for having them.

'British officials ... (together with most of the NATO military establishment) emphasized the need for modernization ... Existing capabilities, all based in the United Kingdom, were ageing and were in need of replacement. Modernization was required *irrespective* of developments in Soviet capabilities. The SS-20 was not essential to this argument ... However, in the public discussion, attention increasingly focused on the SS-20 because it is easier to discuss publicly the need for LRTNF (Long-Range Theatre Nuclear Force) modernization by pointing to visible Soviet capabilities than by explaining somewhat esoteric NATO doctrine' (our italics).[2] The 'esoteric' doctrine referred to is the NATO doctrine of flexible response.

On 24 January 1983, President Reagan was reported as saying that, without Cruise and Pershing II, Western Europe would be left 'without one weapon of a deterrent nature'.[3] This ignores the existence of Polaris, Poseidon, French weapons and US and RAF nuclear bombers! The main justification for Cruise is therefore totally invalid. But there are in addition many other arguments against the cruise missile.

### Dual key or no dual key?

First of all, the cruise missiles destined for Europe will be launched entirely by US personnel. There will be no British, Dutch, Belgian, German or Italian fingers on the buttons. This represents a marked departure from the procedure adopted for other NATO missiles currently deployed in Europe (and for the old 'Thor' missiles once based in East Anglia) – short-range 'Lance' missiles, for example, now in service with the British Army of the Rhine, are operated under a dual control system. Britain bought the missiles from the United States and therefore technically owns them. Although

British personnel actually man the launchers, the warheads for these missiles are under the direct control of US personnel. Both parties must therefore be involved in the launch procedure. This so-called 'dual control' or 'dual key' system ensures that both nations have to participate jointly in firing the missiles – one of them cannot do it alone. The United States originally insisted on this safeguard as a condition on the export of nuclear missiles to its NATO partners. There will be no such safeguard with cruise missiles, however, and although they will be based on European soil they will be under US ownership and launched solely by US servicemen.

Mrs Thatcher's government has fended off criticism of the lack of a dual key system by stating that the use of cruise missiles would be a matter of 'joint decision in the light of the circumstances prevailing at the time' by the British and United States governments.

Historically, records show that successive US governments have consistently refused to guarantee consultation over the use of US weapons deployed on British soil.[4] Admiral Gene La Rocque, a former deputy head of the Pentagon's strategic plans division, has said that 'the British government's insistence that the use of cruise missiles based in Britain would be a matter for joint Anglo–American decision amounted to bureaucratic obfuscation ... the decision to use nuclear weapons in Europe is purely a US decision. One of the great myths that's been perpetrated in Europe is that somehow the NATO countries ... will have something to say about whether the US uses nuclear weapons. They will not ... There's nobody in Europe that could stop us.'[5]

Defence Secretary Michael Heseltine has pointed out that RAF personnel would be responsible for guarding the Cruise TEL convoys, thereby exercising some control over them. This is not dual control however, because the USA will not allow these RAF personnel to be involved in the launching procedure.[6] Michael Heseltine has stated that Britain could only get dual control by effectively buying the cruise missiles from the United States at a cost of £1,000,000,000 which he argues is economically unjustified.

On balance it appears that European host nations will have no effective control over the launch of the new cruise missiles. This could have serious consequences for Britain and raises some basic questions. Can we always be sure that the United States will not use these missiles in circumstances when we wouldn't wish to use them ourselves? Can we always be sure that the United States will act in our best interests rather than in its own? The truth of the matter is that US and British interests do not *always* coincide and for this reason the deployment of cruise missiles in Britain is tantamount to relinquishing national sovereignty.

## First strike

A further objection to cruise missiles is that they have such high accuracy that they could be used to destroy hardened-concrete rocket silos and thus potentially not for deterrence but for fighting a nuclear war. In principle, cruise missiles are 'slow and stealthy' – they fly low to avoid ground radar detection and can fly a devious route to achieve an element of surprise. There has been much debate about whether they have a 'first-strike capability' – that is the ability to knock out Soviet missiles and command bunkers in a disarming surprise attack to gain a major military advantage. Cruise missiles certainly have the required accuracy and explosive yield to destroy enemy missiles but ground-launched versions in Europe will not be introduced in sufficient numbers to destroy the main Soviet ICBM force.

However large numbers of air-launched cruise missiles (with the same accuracy and first-strike potential) are being deployed on B-52 (and forthcoming B-1) bombers, both in Europe and the US. In a few years, when 'stealth' cruise missiles and bombers, virtually undetectable to radar, become available, the total force of air-, ground- and sea-launched cruise missiles, plus the other weapons of high accuracy, may then have a first-strike capability against the Soviet Union. The trend towards 'first strike' is a major destabilizing factor in world security.

## Limited nuclear war and flexible response

NATO plans for the use of cruise missiles within the strategy of flexible response are also disquieting. In this strategy – which is quite different to the old concept of deterrence by mutually assured destruction – NATO would fight a nuclear war in stages of deliberate escalation. Each threatened stage of escalation is supposed to deter further escalation by the other side. NATO plans to use cruise missiles as one stage of this 'flexible response' to supposedly deter further escalation to all-out nuclear war.

Even without the existence of the new missiles, such as cruise and Pershing II, it is hardly credible that this strategy could ever work. Each side would have to withhold using larger weapons and risk their possible destruction before they were used. Even if commanders were able to keep detailed control of their forces there would probably be a staged escalation culminating in full-scale nuclear war. Far more likely, military communication would be disrupted at an early stage, at which point local commanders would let fly with all the weapons at their disposal.

With the new highly accurate weapons, which are supposedly linked, bolstering the flexible response, the strategy is even less likely to work. Once cruise and Pershing II missiles were fired, the Soviet Union would almost certainly respond by firing their strategic weapons to avoid their being destroyed in their silos. Thus the firing of cruise and Pershing II, far from limiting the scale of the nuclear war, would almost certainly bring about full-scale nuclear war.

## Fuelling the arms race

It is generally accepted that US cruise missile technology (small efficient jet-engines, small warheads with high yields, accurate navigation aids, etc.) is at least ten years ahead of comparable Soviet technology.[7] The production and widespread deployment of cruise missiles necessarily forces the Soviets to develop their own similar technology and to build up their air defences to protect themselves. According to US intelligence reports, the Soviet Union has now developed its own version of a long-range (1500 miles) cruise missile designated the SS-CM-4 which it may decide to deploy on mobile launchers.[8]

The Soviet Union is also building fifty IL-76 airborne early warning aeroplanes (AWACs) to spot incoming cruise missiles and MIG-25 Super Foxbat fighters to shoot them down. The MIG-25s are supersonic (and thus fly faster than current GLCMs) and carry the AA-X-9 guided missile. US intelligence reports have indicated that in tests MIG-25s flying at 20,000 feet have successfully destroyed a number of target missiles flying at 1,000 feet or less.[9] This development is hardly unexpected, but it has been used by the United States to justify the development of the improved 'stealth' cruise missile.

The US pursuit of advanced cruise missile technology is clearly causing a significant explosion in the arms race.

Cruise missiles also pose severe problems for the verification of arms limitations treaties. The long-range strategic version with a nuclear warhead has an identical external appearance to the short-range tactical version with a conventional warhead. This makes them impossible to distinguish by superficial inspection, although bombers carrying air-launched cruise missiles with nuclear warheads are supposed to be labelled by attaching small fins called 'frods' which can be spotted by satellites!

There have been no attempts to control the deployment of cruise missiles by treaty to date, and any future arms control agreements may well founder on the question of cruise verification. The variety of different types does not make control any easier. Also, the relative cheapness (about $1,000,000) of cruise missiles makes them an an attractive proposition for countries which have recently acquired nuclear weapons and are looking for ways to deliver them.

## Target Britain

As far as Britain is concerned, there is one other fundamental objection to the basing of ground-launched cruise missiles at Greenham Common and Molesworth. The TELs could disperse to any location in the Midlands or southern England if a conflict ever broke out, thereby making the UK a launching zone which would have to be heavily bombarded to guarantee destruction of all the GLCMs, because the thick cloud cover prevalent over the UK makes it difficult for them to be accurately pinpointed by satellites. Geoffrey Pattie, Secretary of State for Defence (Air Force), said in a written reply to a question in the House of Commons that 'more than 1000 MT would be needed to destroy the ground-launched cruise missiles once they were dispersed'.[10] This is equivalent to 80,000 times the explosive power of the bomb dropped on Hiroshima. Moreover the actual dispersal of cruise missiles from their home bases in time of tension or during exercises could be interpreted

## Basic Objections to Cruise Missiles in Britain

1. They would be effectively under sole US control. US and UK interests do not always coincide.

2. They are weapons which could be used to fight a so-called 'limited' nuclear war in Europe, thus making all-out nuclear war more likely.

3. Combined air-launched and ground-launched cruise missile forces, in conjunction with other highly accurate missiles, would have a disarming first-strike capability. This upsets the global nuclear stalemate.

4. They fuel the arms race. In response the Soviet Union is upgrading its air defences and developing its own cruise missiles.

5. They defeat easy verification of arms limitation treaties – primarily because tactical conventional versions and strategic nuclear versions look the same.

6. They invite a massive retaliatory attack on England (equivalent to 80,000 Hiroshimas).

7. They are not needed for deterrence, as a massive overkill potential already exists.

as a preparation for war and might precipitate a pre-emptive attack by the Soviet Union.

The arguments above give good cause for doubting the wisdom of positioning cruise missiles in Europe and even for manufacturing them at all. But this is not the end of the matter. The entire Cruise programme is an enigma. The US government must have realized with foresight that any attempt to deploy such weapons in large numbers would force the Russians to upgrade their defences and develop similar technology. In this case why were they ever developed – was it because of vested commercial interests? Was it because, as has been suggested, the technology was there so they had to find a use for it? Does the United States now really expect to maintain a lead in cruise missile technology? It is certainly in a position to be able to do so with the advances to date. Whatever the reasons behind the production and deployment of cruise missiles it is apparent that they are not needed by Britain as a deterrent force – particularly when we will not control them. It is certainly true that the Soviet SS-20s threaten the UK but the sixty-four Polaris missiles in service with the Royal Navy are capable of destroying most of the large Soviet cities – is this not deterrence enough? In addition there is little doubt that cruise missiles are fuelling the arms race and will make verification of arms treaties virtually impossible. In combination with the military strategy of flexible response, they potentially pose unacceptable risks by suggesting that a limited nuclear war in Europe is feasible, making all-out nuclear war more likely. The overwhelming conclusion must be that cruise missiles should not be deployed in any circumstances.

## Pershing II

The US Department of Defense Annual Report to Congress for 1980 states that: 'Pershing II is an improvement to the Pershing IA that it will replace. Pershing II will utilize a new re-entry vehicle, new propulsion stages, and new ground support equipment.'[11] This brief bland statement completely disregards the most important characteristics of Pershing II and fails to recognize any implications for international security other than that it is a more 'effective' weapon.

Yet the Pershing II has some very special features. It has the most accurate guidance system of any ballistic missile in the world and, from its proposed bases in Germany, could penetrate well into Eastern Europe and the Soviet Union within a few minutes of launch. The forty yard accuracy of the Pershing II means that it can reliably knock out a Soviet missile in a hardened-concrete silo. At least four out of five Pershing IIs are likely to destroy their target silos – even with a small ten kiloton warhead.

The speed of these missiles, their accuracy, and their capacity to destroy a silo means that they pose an unacceptable threat to the Soviet missiles in the western part of the USSR. As with cruise, Pershing II is such a highly 'effective' weapon that it adds instability to the nuclear weapons balance and gives rise to added dangers for the West.

Hypothetically, all 108 Pershing II launchers could fire missiles almost simultaneously towards pre-selected missile targets in the Soviet Union. With rapid reloading facilities the remaining 200 Pershing II missiles could also be fired within a short time. If such a surprise attack were ever launched, the Soviets would have to respond very quickly before their command centres and missiles were blown up on the ground. Once the missiles had been detected, there could be as little as two to three minutes to decide on an appropriate response to attack. This brief period gives little or no time for deliberation. For retaliation to occur at all the response would have to be immediate. This very short response time means in practice that the Soviets would have to rely on a largely automatic computer-controlled system to detect an incoming attack and to direct a response. Such a system is commonly known as a 'launch-on-warning' system. The Soviets have already made it clear that they will develop a launch-on-warning system if Pershing II missiles are put into Europe – they can hardly be expected to do otherwise.

Although it can be argued that the West would never launch a first-strike nuclear attack against the USSR, the Soviets themselves can never be absolutely sure about this. They are as fearful of Western intentions as the West is of theirs. A launch-on-warning system is therefore highly likely to be adopted by the Soviet Union as a necessary protection for their vulnerable missiles. This is where the danger lies. Any rapid launch-on-warning system must be primarily automatic – even though people may form the last part of the chain and actually turn the firing keys. Automatic attack detection can be performed by ground-based radar and orbiting satellites which have sensors to spot the flares of rocket plumes as they are launched. The warning information from such sources must be processed rapidly by computer for interpretation and response. But computers do make mistakes and have made mistakes in the past. Any mistake with a quick-reaction launch-on-warning system would release missiles and start World War III. Missiles cannot be recalled once launched.

Of course it is often said that computers don't make mistakes and we are constantly being reassured about this by those who control both nuclear weapons and nuclear power plants. But people who work with computers know that there is much truth in the saying 'To err is human, but for a real cock-up you need a computer.' The reasons for this are quite clear. A computer is a machine which executes a sequence of pre-programmed instructions. These instructions are normally followed very precisely and extremely rapidly. A computer can be a real benefit and work efficiently through calculations in a few minutes that would take the human brain several years. But the computer is not human. It is only capable of following specified instructions. It has no intuition, and never has second thoughts. It is a man-made automaton which is only as good as its designer and programmer. If its program contains mistakes (even one as small as a comma being misprinted as a full-stop) it could yield quite unexpected results. If it were presented with unusual information in circumstances which had not been foreseen by the programmer it could arrive at the wrong conclusions. This is the danger of reliance on computers.

Historically there have been several occurrences of computer error leading to disaster. In fact this happened in the Falklands conflict in 1982. Several British warships equipped with sophisticated electronic surveillance and defence systems were sunk by Argentinian Exocet missiles. At the time it was thought that the surveillance systems simply could not detect low-flying surface-skimming missiles and take defensive action. Some months later, however, it emerged that the ship-board computers had correctly detected the incoming missiles and even identified them but had not ordered defensive measures (such as releasing radar decoy material) because they had been programmed to accept the French-built Exocet as friendly.[12] The programmers had not envisaged a situation in which missiles built by a NATO country would be used to attack British ships. The unexpected happened and disaster was the result. In the context of nuclear warfare with computerized launch-on-warning the disaster could be the end of European civilization. The time factor is critical. If there is insufficient time for human intervention to check if an attack has been diagnosed correctly, the danger of nuclear war starting by accident is greatly increased. The Pershing II missiles' combination of speed, short flight-time, and accuracy will necessitate a 'hair-trigger' response which increases the likelihood of accidental nuclear war – particularly as Soviet computer technology is believed to be less reliable than Western computer technology. For this reason Pershing II should not be deployed in Europe. President Kennedy refused to allow the siting of intermediate-range Soviet missiles in Cuba in 1962 for similar reasons. (The distance between Cuba and Washington D.C. is similar to the distance between West Germany and Moscow.)

As with Cruise, it is worth inquiring why NATO sees it as so important to deploy Pershing II. Because of the massive overkill potential which already exists, these missiles are certainly not needed for deterrence. Have they been built for military reasons, for purely commercial reasons, or to accelerate a technology lead over the USSR? The answer has not been forthcoming – but the objection is clear enough.

## The SS-20s and the Reagan and Andropov proposals

Over three hundred SS-20s have now been deployed of which two thirds are targeted on western Europe, and the remaining third on China. They each carry three independently targetable warheads, and in total the force comprises enough warheads to strike at about 1000 separate targets within Europe or continental Asia. This force is far greater than that needed for deterrence against China and the European countries of NATO; it is also quite separate from the long-range intercontinental force targeted on the USA.

Table 1 opposite shows the numbers of 'theatre' nuclear missiles in Eurasia at the beginning of 1983, prior to the planned introduction of Cruise and Pershing II (SIPRI and UN numbers and classifications).[13]

In November 1981 the United States and the Soviet Union opened negotiations in Geneva on the reduction of European nuclear missiles. So far little progress has been made, and both sides have come up with proposals which the other has felt unable to accept. There have been three main proposals: Reagan's 'zero option', the 'Andropov proposals' and Reagan's recent 'compromise' proposal.

Reagan's much publicized zero option calls for the dismantling of all SS-4, SS-5 and SS-20 missiles in return for which NATO will not deploy Cruise or Pershing II missiles in Europe. In Soviet eyes this proposal is unrealistic because it takes no account of the British, French and Chinese forces which are targeted against them. These forces are also likely to rise sharply in the next few years, particularly if the new French M-4s and Britain's proposed Trident D-5 are deployed. In fact, the Americans and the other NATO countries have consistently refused to allow these forces to be counted in any agreements. From the Soviet point of view, Reagan's recent 'compromise' proposals (less GLCMs and Pershing IIs in return for less SS-20s) are just as unreasonable and also take no account of different weapon capabilities.

The Andropov proposals put forward in early 1983 specified a reduction in the SS-20 force to 162 missiles in return for no Cruise or Pershing II. In NATO eyes this Soviet proposal is unrealistic because the missiles would not be dismantled but simply be moved east of the Urals. Their mobility means that they could be brought back to the western side of the Soviet Union if required. Secondly, NATO argues that the 162 SS-20s match the British and French forces in missile total only, and not in numbers of independently targetable warheads.

These recent Andropov and Reagan proposals are very good examples of why arms control talks have failed dismally over the last thirty-eight years. By excluding different categories of

| Country | Missile | Year first deployed | Range (miles) | Accuracy (yards) | Warheads | No. of missiles | No. of targets that can be hit |
|---|---|---|---|---|---|---|---|
| USSR | SS-4 | 1959 | 1100 | 2400 | 1×1MT | 350 | 350 |
| | SS-5 | 1961 | 2200 | 1200 | 1×1MT | 333 | 999 |
| | SS-20 | 1976 | 3000 | 400 | 3×150 kT† | 18 | 18 |
| | SS-N-5 | 1963 | 750 | ? | 1× MT? | | |
| USA | Pershing II | 1983 | 1100 | 40 | up to 250 kT | (311)[a] | (311) |
| | GLCM | 1983 | 1500 | 50 | up to 200 kT | (464) | (464) |
| UK | Polaris A-3 (with Chevaline warheads) | 1967 | 2800 | 800 | 6×50 kT* | 64 | 64 |
| | Trident D-5 | 1990? | 6000 | 250 | 10×335 kT† | (64)? | (640) |
| France | SSBS S-3 | 1980 | 1800 | ? | 1×1MT | 18 | 18 |
| | MSBS M-20 | 1977 | 1800 | ? | 1×1MT | 80 | 80 |
| | MSBS M-4 | 1985? | 2500 | ? | 6×150 kT* | (96) | (96) |
| China | CSS-3 | 1976 | 4300 | ? | ? | 2? | |
| | CSS-2 | ? | 1600 | ? | ? | 50-70 | |
| | CSS-1 | ? | 600 | ? | ? | 40-50 | 120? |

Numbers shown in brackets indicate missiles yet to be deployed

[a] 311 planned for 108 launchers

† = multiple warheads (independently targetable – MIRV)

* = multiple warheads (only one target – MRV)

In addition to the weapons shown many other missiles have been assigned for European targeting such as the Soviet SS-11, SS-19 and SS-N-5s on Hotel-II submarines, and 400 warheads on American Poseidon submarine-launched missiles which have been allocated to SACEUR (the commander of NATO forces in Europe). There are also many shorter range nuclear missiles.

*Table 1.* Theatre nuclear missiles in Eurasia (for data sources see note 13).

weapons both sides can juggle with the figures in Table 1 to produce an apparent advantage for either side.

Rationality demands that both sides should reduce their forces. The West, for their part, should acknowledge that the British and French forces do have some bearing on Soviet security. Bilateral US–USSR talks about forces in Europe cannot be carried on in a vacuum, as though Britain and France did not exist – particularly as they are both allied to NATO.

The Soviet Union should acknowledge that simply moving some SS-20s east of the Urals is inadequate. If common sense is to prevail, there is a need for more than mere self-interest. The attitudes of the superpowers and many European governments are inexcusable. It is high time for the European governments to accept their share of the responsibility for the current situation and no longer let themselves be pawns in the game of the superpowers. Playing the nuclear numbers game is really missing the point. Each side could destroy the other many times over. Unilateral reductions in nuclear weapons would be a trust-building exercise which could only lead to greater mutual security.

## Trident

In July 1980 the Conservative government announced that it had provisionally decided to buy the American built Trident C-4 submarine missile system to replace the four Polaris submarines as Britain's nuclear deterrent. These new Trident missiles have been developed by the United States to replace their own Polaris and Poseidon missiles. The Trident missiles have longer range than the others and also greater accuracy. In June 1981 it was revealed that the cost of the new system to Britain would be about £6,000,000,000. By February 1982 it was decided to buy a newer version, Trident D-5, the cost of which was then estimated at £7,500,000,000. The government now intends to buy this system for operational use in the 1990s despite much opposition.

The proposed Trident system represents a considerable increase in destructive power over the Polaris system. Table 2 shows the difference between the two. It is planned that Britain will buy four Trident submarines each equipped with sixteen missiles –

| | Polaris<br>(with Chevaline) | Trident D–5† |
|---|---|---|
| Total no. of submarines | 4 | 4 |
| Total no. of missiles | 64 | 64 |
| No. of warheads per missile | 6 | 10 |
| Explosive power per warhead | 50 kT | up to 335 kT |
| Total explosive power | 19·2 MT | 214.4 MT |
| Total no. of separate targets that can be attacked | 64 | 640 |
| Area which can be devastated* | 2590 sq. miles | up to 7828 sq. miles |

* Area over which blast pressure would exceed 5psi (sufficient to destroy brick structures such as British housing). Lighter damage and lethal fall-out will cover many
times this area. Figures assume bombs are ground-burst and damage zones do not
overlap.

† The data in this column is based on the believed specification of Britain's proposed
system. The system is not to become operational until the 1990s and the precise
characteristics may be subject to amendment. Trident submarines can carry up to 24
missiles each with up to 14 warheads per missile.

*Table 2.* Some numerical comparisons between Britain's existing Polaris force and
the proposed Trident submarine missile system.

the same number as the existing Polaris force. The big difference,
however, is the total number of warheads and their explosive yields.
Each Polaris missile can only hit one target, whereas each
Trident missile can hit ten. The six Chevaline warheads on each
Polaris are not independently targetable and would fall in the same
target zone. The Trident warheads however are completely
independently targetable, thus boosting the total number of ground
targets that can be attacked by a factor of ten. The total area of
territory which can be devastated by the Trident system is also
much greater than the area which can be devastated by Polaris.
In all these respects the Trident force represents a substantial
escalation in Britain's nuclear capability.

Defence Secretary Michael Heseltine has stated[14] that Britain needs to purchase the Trident system with its extra warheads because of improvements in Soviet missile defences. This argument falls down in many respects. In the first place, as allowed under the SALT-1 treaty, the USSR has only one anti-ballistic missile system which rings Moscow, and the number of missiles has recently been reduced from sixty-four to thirty-two. Cities such as Leningrad, Minsk and Kiev are unprotected. Secondly, the Chevaline warhead now being deployed on Polaris was developed at great cost specifically to defeat the anti-ballistic missile system.

Quite apart from these points, Trident represents a gross escalation in the European nuclear balance, at a time when arms control in Europe is desperately needed. The Polaris submarine force already gives a significant deterrent threat to any hostile nation (even one the size of the USSR or the USA). The Trident system is also extremely expensive and will probably have cost well over £10,000,000,000 by the time it becomes operational.

It is interesting to note that Trident and Cruise show up a contradiction in the British government's posture. The Trident system is intended to be (as Polaris currently is) an 'independent deterrent force'. In other words Britain anticipates that it may need to use its nuclear force *outside the NATO context* i.e. without US consent. In pro-Cruise arguments, however, the government expects us to accept that US controlled ground-launched cruise missiles on British soil will only be used *within the NATO context* i.e. with British consent. This fundamental contradiction is not explained in the official presentation of the case for the new weapons.

## Battlefield nuclear weapons

Over one half of the estimated 50,000 nuclear warheads in the world are classified as battlefield or tactical weapons. The majority of these are based in Europe – most in Germany on either side of the East–West border. The term 'battlefield nuclear weapons' has actually come to mean many things. Generally speaking, battlefield nuclear weapons are weapons of short range (say less than about 100 miles) which could in theory be used in a localized conflict between armies. The battlefield weapons are thus seen as an integral component of 'flexible response'. Any armed incursion into Western Europe would, in principle, be met by an 'appropriate' use of force, beginning with conventional weapons followed by the battlefield nuclear weapons if the conventional battle were being lost. NATO is fully prepared to be the first to use nuclear weapons in just such a context.

The battlefield or tactical nuclear weapons come in several forms – there are nuclear shells which can be fired by artillery, short-range ballistic missiles (e.g. Lance), bombs for aircraft to carry (e.g. the American F-111 bombers based in Britain and Europe and the RAF Tornado aircraft), and atomic demolition mines – a misnomer, as many of them could 'demolish' an entire city. Many of the NATO M-109 and M-110 Howitzers based in Germany are 'dual capable' – able to fire either conventional or nuclear shells. The Warsaw Pact also has dual capable Howitzers and mortars.

Any use of nuclear weapons in Europe as a battlefield tactic would result in much 'collateral damage' to towns and cities and result in heavy loss of life amongst the civilian population. Battlefield nuclear weapons generally have explosive yields of a few kilotons which is by no means insubstantial. The Hiroshima bomb which killed over 100,000 people would be classified as a battlefield weapon by modern standards. It has been estimated that in a restricted battlefield nuclear confrontation in Europe, involving the use of 200 weapons of 100 kilotons yield and 1500 of a few kilotons yield, the total civilian casualties would amount to six or seven millions, outnumbering the military casualties by a factor of twelve to one.[15]

Furthermore, there is no guarantee that such a small-scale limited tactical nuclear war would actually remain limited. It seems highly unlikely that the use of battlefield nuclear weapons could ever stop a conflict. In fact they are more likely to escalate it. This has been reiterated time and time again by many senior military thinkers, including the late Lord Mountbatten: 'The belief that nuclear weapons ... could be used in field warfare without triggering an all-out nuclear exchange leading to the final holocaust is more and more incredible.'[16] But NATO in particular refuses to heed the warning. NATO considers itself to be conventionally outnumbered in Europe and uses this as a justification for deploying battlefield nuclear weapons and for producing the enhanced radiation weapon (the neutron bomb – see Appendix 1). Independent analyses indicate however that such a disparity does not really exist.[17] To take just one much vaunted fact, the Warsaw Pact tank superiority is more than adequately balanced by NATO's conventional and highly effective anti-tank rockets.

Above all the deployment of battlefield nuclear weapons in Europe so close to the East–West border could lead to an early breach of the nuclear threshold in any conflict, from which there may be no going back. This danger has been lucidly stated by the Independent Commission on Disarmament and Security Issues: 'Because of their deployment in forward areas, battlefield nuclear weapons run the risk of being over-run early in an armed conflict. Maintaining command and control over such weapons in "the fog of war" would be difficult. Pressures for delegation of authority to use nuclear weapons to local commanders and for their early use would be strong. The danger of crossing the nuclear threshold and of further escalation could become acute. It should be remembered in this connection that the areas close to the East–West border in Central Europe are densely populated and contain large industrial concentrations.'[18] The Commission went on to advocate a battlefield-nuclear-weapon-free zone as an immediate measure to improve European security. Such a move is badly needed as an urgent interim measure though ideally all such weapons should be removed from Europe. Field Marshal Lord Carver (a former Chief of Defence Staff) has written: 'The urgent need is for NATO to abandon the concept that it can avert conventional defeat by initiating nuclear war: it would only result in an even greater defeat.'[19]

## Conclusion

Beyond any reasonable doubt the case against Cruise, Pershing II, the SS-20s, Trident, and all battlefield nuclear weapons (including the neutron bomb) is unassailable. All of these weapons can be dispensed with unilaterally without reducing the security of the USA, the USSR or Europe in the slightest. Indeed their disposal would improve security for all nations. These new weapons add grave new dangers to a world already massively overpopulated with over 50,000 nuclear warheads and only bring the day of the ultimate holocaust closer. Arguments about comparability at all possible levels of response have no real relevance to the overwhelming dangers that face us all in view of the massive overkill potential in existence. Schemes for fighting limited or battlefield nuclear war only make Armageddon more likely not less likely. Now is the time for the first steps to be taken towards a safer world – with fewer weapons not more weapons. This is the over-riding conclusion which must come from any rational inquiry into the new missiles, regardless of political viewpoint.

# CHAPTER 5

# Perceptions and Propaganda

The West, including the USA, the NATO alliance and other non-aligned West European countries, and the East, including the USSR and the Warsaw Pact countries, are heavily engaged in a propaganda war. Each side reacts to the other's propaganda. The propaganda may be directed internally towards its own people or it may be directed externally towards people in other countries, or both. For example, Western internal propaganda directed towards NATO alliance countries emphasizes the apparent 'imbalance' in nuclear arsenals – a good example of this is 'Reagan's Black and White Missile Show'[1] (see Figure 10). Four white US missiles are shown opposing thirteen black Soviet missiles.

This array of Soviet and US missiles is being used by the Pentagon to show that the USSR is ahead in the missile race and to justify President Reagan's decision to go ahead with the new MX missile. It is, however, interesting primarily for what it does *not* show. Total numbers of missiles and warheads are ignored. No submarine-launched missiles are included, yet the US has 4768 submarine-launched warheads, while the USSR has only 1494.[2] No cruise missiles are shown, yet about 1500 are being deployed on US B-52 bombers. Further, the Soviet SS-16 missile was never deployed, and two earlier experimental versions of the US Minuteman missile, deployed in 1963, are not shown.

Not only is objective information as regards the number of

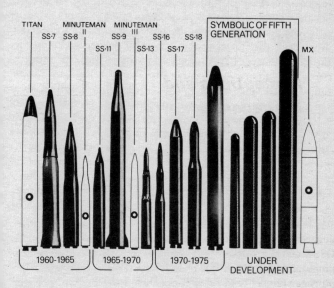

*Figure 10.* Reagan's Black and White Missile Show

missiles lacking, but the 'good' versus 'evil' symbolism of 'white' versus 'black' is fully exploited.

An example of propaganda disseminated not only between countries but also within countries is provided by official government responses to the growth of peace movements in the Eastern and Western blocs. The West accuses the KGB of supporting and funding CND and other peace groups,[3] while, for their part, the USSR claims that unofficial peace groups are supported and encouraged by the CIA![4] Obviously, both sides are highly suspicious of their peace movements.

What is clear is that the propaganda reinforces entrenched positions and prevents any true dialogue. For example, in the UK we are witnessing a concentrated propaganda campaign to counter, diffuse and discredit the peace efforts of CND and other groups – particularly their opposition to the deployment of cruise missiles in the UK, and Pershing II in Europe. Michael Heseltine recently reflected this attitude when he refused to debate with CND, 'for their minds are closed'. In addition, in an attempt to counter CND, the government seriously considered spending £1,000,000 in its campaign to make the new missiles appear essential for Britain's defence.[5] This proposal produced such a storm of opposition that it was withdrawn. Nevertheless government funding has always been available to the British Atlantic Committee, an organization which promotes the NATO viewpoint – giving talks at schools, for example. The Conservative Central Office, and particularly via Winston Churchill MP, have however also helped distribute pamphlets produced by the Coalition for Peace through Security who, according to Adam Raphael of the *Observer*,[6] have engaged in 'a rather squalid and not very intelligent smear' of the CND organization, labelling them as 'Communists, Neutralists and Defeatists' and transposing their famous logo with the Soviet hammer and sickle.

It is important to recognize that the current surge in official propaganda is in part a response by the government to the current surge in the peace movements. It must be remembered, however, that official nuclear propaganda has been produced over the past three decades and has acquired some respectability and credibility. The assumptions underlying the propaganda are rarely exposed to any real scrutiny. It is therefore the aim of this chapter to examine the assumptions and arguments upon which official propaganda is based.

## Jargon

Part of the machinery of propaganda is the replacement of clear and objective description by emotionally appealing or 'cute' phrases. For example, 'Little Boy' and 'Fat Man' were used to describe the bombs dropped on Hiroshima and Nagasaki. Often the language of propaganda embodies a fundamental contradiction; for example, in the phrase, 'Father of the bomb', applied to its inventor, father conjures up the image of life creation, while the bomb is a weapon of mass destruction. The term 'Cookie Cutter' has been used to describe the neutron bomb, which supposedly kills people, leaving buildings intact (although this is not the case and the neutron bomb is highly destructive in its own right).

Another technique (in some ways the reverse of the above) is to use apparently technical or scientific terms to describe something which is emotionally very unappealing. The term 'Nukespeak' has been coined for this technique.[7] There are numerous examples, such as '100 per cent mortality response', which means 'everybody is dead', 'demographic targeting', which means obliteration of large cities and 'collateral damage', which means devastation of large areas of countryside, including trees, crops, livestock and people, as an unavoidable by-product of fighting a nuclear war. A widely used phrase is 'limited nuclear war', which means the obliteration of Europe in a war between the superpowers, with tens of millions dead.

## Who is the aggressor?

The overall military and economic strategy of a country (offensive, defensive or neutral) can be measured by the number of direct or indirect military and economic confrontations in which it is involved throughout the world. It is constantly claimed by the West that the USSR is the aggressor. Various military involvements are cited – the invasion of Afghanistan, Hungary and Czechoslovakia – together with economic and political involvements including Poland, Pakistan, Cuba, Vietnam and African Nationalist movements. The justifications for the West's fear and paranoia about Soviet expansionism have been questioned. For example, according to retired US Rear-Admiral Gene La Rocque: 'It just baffles me how we have developed this paranoia about the Soviets. The Soviets are in six relatively unimportant countries today. They're in Angola, Mozambique, Ethiopia, Cuba, Afghanistan and South Yemen, none of which is important, and all of which cost the Soviet Union money and resources every day. Then, take a look at the Soviet Union over the past thirty years and look at the places they've been kicked out of. They've been kicked out of Indonesia, the sixth largest nation in the world, kicked out of China, kicked out of Egypt, and kicked out of Somalia, where they had their only naval base outside of the Soviet Union. I think our fear of the Soviets is based on lack of information and total absence of any factual data. If you look at the success of the Soviets as imperialists, they are flops. They are not strong around the world.'[8]

What are not often cited with the same clarity and intensity are the various Western military involvements, for example, Korea, Vietnam, Cuba, Iran, El Salvador, Nicaragua and the various political and economic activities in Chile, Greece, Argentina, Somalia and other parts of Africa.

In terms of opposing ideologies, the West point to the Soviet Union's Marxist–Leninist doctrine, Communist expansionism, and the goal of world domination; the Soviets cite the West's Imperialist aggression and pro-capitalist stance. Such propaganda arguments are at best superficial; in reality, each side is engaged in a power struggle to maintain its spheres of influence and extend its own interests.

There are several historical points which are relevant to understanding how the world was divided up after World War II into 'spheres of influence' and how the Soviet Union entered into the arms race. It should be remembered that:

1. The Soviet Union was an ally to the West and lost twenty million people in the Second World War, whereas Britain lost one quarter of a million soldiers.
2. Because of the USA's late entry into the war and since the US mainland was not invaded, it emerged virtually unscathed from the Second World War with a rapidly expanding industrial and economic base.
3. The obvious threat to Soviet security following the bombing of Hiroshima and Nagasaki led to the start of the arms race.
4. The Truman/Churchill/Stalin 'division' of the world after the Second World War recognized the Soviet Union's need for a protective zone of buffer states between themselves and Germany. However, the annexation of Poland and the other East European states did not seem justifiable to those annexed and has led to much tension within the Warsaw Pact.

From a broader viewpoint, taking into account military and economic involvement, both the USA and the USSR can be seen as aggressors. They are not, as so often stated, each simply responding to the 'enemy'.

## Who has weapons superiority?

It is constantly claimed that the West lags behind the Eastern bloc in terms of conventional and nuclear weapons and that, in order to bridge the gap, increased defence expenditure is justified. Such a claim is all the justification needed to fuel the quest for ever more sophisticated technology, thus perpetuating the arms race.

It is claimed, for example, that in Europe the Soviet Union has a vast superiority in tanks – poised to invade West Germany or Poland, perhaps. Although this may be numerically correct, what is not stated is that the Western modern anti-tank weapons are more than adequate to quell such an invasion by the rather aged Soviet tank force. 'Thus, whereas the West has a $1:2\frac{1}{2}$ inferiority in main battle tanks in the Ministry of Defence's much reproduced histogram, by 1978 NATO had in place 200,000 precision-guided munitions and 17,000 launchers, which gives better than a 10:1 superiority in precision-guided anti-tank weapons over Warsaw Pact tanks.'[9] In addition, the NATO tanks are considered far superior by the West. This is just one example. A detailed analysis of the weapons arsenals overall reveals that, because of the many different types, delivery, accuracy, megatonnage and range of weapons, working out who is 'ahead' is extremely complex.

One side may be made to appear inferior by comparing like categories but simultaneously excluding a portion of a given side's nuclear weapons. To compare weapons, category against category, is misleading and insufficient. If an adequate defence system is required it is necessary also to compare defensive against offensive weapons, e.g. tank versus anti-tank weapons, aircraft versus anti-aircraft weapons.

To the person in the street the precise meaning of nuclear parity or nuclear balance is obscure. In a world filled with over 50,000 nuclear warheads, totalling more than 13,000 MT, and where both sides can deliver over three tons of TNT (equivalent) for every man, woman and child on this planet – what is the meaning of nuclear balance? If we can kill the Russians twenty-five times over and they us thirty times over, who is ahead? The so-called argument for nuclear balance, the numbers game, by its very nature fuels the arms race, despite the unprecedented dangers that further arming implies.

## Deterrence

In government propaganda the possession of a 'credible deterrent' is seen as absolutely essential for the 'defence' of the West against the USSR. Yet the notion of nuclear deterrence in the West is quite different from that in the Soviet Union. 'For years, the Soviet Ministry of Defence dictionary had no entry at all for "deterrence" and under "nuclear deterrence" gave not a translation but an explanatory sentence. More recently the Soviet military have created a special word ... which represents the western concept of deterrence and is used only for that purpose.'[10] In other words no equivalent concept to the Western one of deterrence existed in the Soviet Union.

In the West the concept of nuclear deterrence is divided into two parts. The first is based on the idea that nuclear war may be deterred or prevented by fear. This is the reason for targeting large cities. The second part is distinct and is considered as 'defence'. This includes the idea of 'flexible response' and the idea of fighting a 'limited'-scale nuclear war. Soviet military strategists do not attempt to separate the concept of 'defence' from the concept of 'deterrence'. In Soviet military theory, a limited nuclear war would inevitably escalate into a fight to the finish and would not be 'limited' in any sense[11] – a point we have already made elsewhere. Since the concepts of nuclear deterrence differ between the USA and the USSR, it is a grave mistake for Western theorists to interpret Soviet intentions in terms of Western military doctrine and vice versa.

## Examples of nuclear propaganda

### How to deal with a bully (Figure 11)

This is a Ministry of Defence publication which is available free to interested individuals and to schools. It seems likely that it is schoolchildren who will be most affected by this; to them the idea of 'dealing with a bully' is particularly close. Interestingly it contains most of the major propaganda arguments appearing in other official Ministry of Defence and Foreign Office publications.

The first image this pamphlet presents is of a small British bulldog (complete with Union Jack) confronting a snarling bear. The message this image is supposed to convey is then spelled out: 'Many of us have had to stand up to a bully at some stage in our lives. The only answer is to say: "Let me alone – or you'll be sorry." And to have the strength to back up your words. The situation *is just the same* between Russia and the West' (our italics). That is to say, the USSR (or snarling bear) is labelled, by implication, as aggressive and offensive; the UK (or sturdy bulldog), on the other hand, is depicted as resolute and defensive.

The pamphlet goes on to say, 'Strength and deterrence. That's the way to secure peace – not wishful thinking.' We are thus led into equating our individual emotional response to a bully with the nation's deterrence doctrine, into considering in terms of playground conflict a conflict which threatens our planet with nuclear annihilation. Thus the assertion in the pamphlet that the 'only' response to a 'bully' is 'Let me alone – or you'll be sorry' encourages us to draw the false parallel that the only correct way of responding to a threat is by a counter-threat.

At present the world is being threatened by two major 'bullies' – the USSR and the USA. Both carry a big nuclear stick. Neither wants any minor bullies to acquire similar nuclear sticks – hence their resistance to the spread of nuclear weapons. Little attempt is made to achieve any mutual understanding or dialogue.

Another major claim in this pamphlet is: 'NATO's policy of deterrence has kept peace in Europe for over thirty years – that's a history lesson none of us can afford to ignore.' Although there may be a correlation between the possession of nuclear weapons and the absence of war in Europe since the Second World War, such a correlation is no proof; the absence of war may have been for various other reasons – the relative political stability of Europe during this period, for example.

Following the US bombing of Hiroshima and Nagasaki, the world was divided up into spheres of influence. Once the spheres of influence were established in which Western Europe was subject

*Figure 11.*

to US power and Eastern Europe subject to Soviet power, it was mutually advantageous for both sides to stay within their own areas and thus avoid conflict. It is therefore more likely that it is this rather than deterrence that has kept the peace. Moreover, even if we were to allow that deterrence has kept the peace for a certain time it does not follow that it can continue to do so, especially given the quality and quantity of the new weapons. These weapons, by their very nature, imply first-strike capability and therefore raise questions about the official defensive posture of deterrence.

As pointed out earlier, deterrence has undergone a radical change as a result of changing Western military strategy arising from the new weapons technology. If deterrence has kept the peace for so long, as the government claims, why has it been necessary to develop a new generation of nuclear weapons?

## Cruise missiles

The Ministry of Defence has recently produced a glossy folder entitled 'Cruise Missiles – A Vital Part of the West's Life Insurance'. This folder has been distributed free to all householders living near to the proposed cruise missile sites at Greenham Common and Molesworth.

A central part of the government case is presented in the bar chart which is reproduced in Figure 12. This shows the balance of 'longer-ranged land-based theatre nuclear forces at the end of 1979'. The data contained in this bar chart is, however, selective and hence highly misleading. The term 'longer-ranged' in this context means that hundreds of land-based nuclear missiles on both sides (such as US/NATO Pershing IA, Lance and Honest Johns; Russian SS-1, SS-12, SS-21 and Frog 7s; and the French Pluton missiles) with ranges less than the Russian SS-4 missile

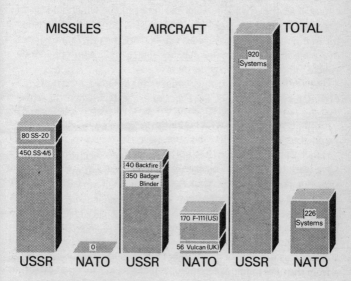

*Figure 12.* The MOD bar-chart: 'The balance of longer-ranged land-based theatre nuclear forces at the end of 1979'

are excluded. Furthermore, several thousand nuclear artillery shells possessed by both sides are ignored.

The term 'land-based' means that all the submarine-launched missiles possessed by both sides are not included. This excludes the UK's 'deterrent' force of Polaris A-3, the French MSBS M-20, US Poseidon submarines allocated to Europe and the Soviet SS-N-5 submarine-launched missiles. (Exactly the same misleading technique is used in a Foreign Office wall-chart designed for schools entitled 'Arms Control and Disarmament'.)

The term 'theatre' means that in addition over a thousand intercontinental-range land-based and submarine-launched missiles possessed by both sides are ignored. In this category the West has a greater number of warheads.

Clearly, the bar chart does not show anything like the full nuclear picture and falsely implies the complete absence of a NATO deterrent missile force, whereas in fact several thousand warheads are aimed at the Soviet Union.

The final comparison of total 'systems' is not meaningful because of all the excluded categories of weapons, which add up to several thousand on each side. In any case, do such comparisons mean anything when both sides can destroy the other many times over? What is the advantage of being able to make your opponent's rubble jump higher than your own?

The cruise missile document makes many other assertions, all of which support the NATO belief that the deployment of cruise missiles within the strategy of 'flexible response' strengthens deterrence by making the threat of the *use* of nuclear weapons more credible.

They argue that Polaris missiles are unusable because 'we could be faced with two stark choices – surrender or all-out nuclear war'; thus the *use* of Polaris is clearly equated with all-out nuclear war, while Cruise is not. (Exactly the same argument is presented in the Ministry of Defence slide-show – 'A Better Road to Peace'.) This argument is completely contradictory because the total destructive power of the Cruise force ($160 \times 200$ kT $= 32,000$ kT) is far more than the Polaris force fitted with the new Chevaline warheads ($64 \times 300$ kT $= 19,200$ kT)! Yet cruise missiles are sold as 'A Vital Part of the West's Life Insurance', and NATO plans to *use* these weapons 'to persuade the Russian leadership – even at the eleventh hour – to draw back'. So to use the NATO argument the cruise missiles would be just as unusable as Polaris, we are still faced with the same 'stark choice' and the whole NATO strategy of 'flexible response' is undermined.

## The media and the 'human chain'

On Good Friday 1983, CND organized a 14-mile human chain linking three sites of special significance to the nuclear debate in Berkshire's 'nuclear valley'. These were the Royal Ordnance Factory at Burghfield where nuclear warheads are believed to be assembled, the Atomic Weapons Research Establishment at Aldermaston, and the cruise missile base at Greenham Common. Estimates of the total number of protesters ranged from 40,000 to 80,000 – the Police estimate is the lower one, CND's the higher.

The following day (2 April 1983) the national newspapers all gave high prominence to the protest but naturally all gave their individual interpretation. It is interesting to examine the way in which the well-ordered peaceful protest was reported, particularly the 'selective' reporting of only those aspects of the event which were consistent with the impression the newspaper wanted to create.

It consisted, in reality, of ordinary people from all walks of life and from all parts of Britain who had given up part of their Easter holiday to express their dissatisfaction with the arms race, though this was not, in many cases, the impression given.

The *Daily Mirror*, for example, reported that the men 'were swathed in chunky-knit sweaters, the type worn in smart Hampstead pubs where they serve real ale'. It went on to report that 'there were splinter groups of every imaginable fragment. There were Lesbians Against the Bomb, Vegetarians Against the Bomb, Single Parent Families Against the Bomb ...' It was a striking feature of the *Mirror*'s report that the descriptions of the various types of demonstrator bore little resemblance to the typical *Daily Mirror* reader. They were clearly, in the *Mirror* reporter's eyes, an alien bunch.

The *Daily Express* report was dominated by government statements and official 'information'. It reported for example that the Police operation for the day cost £120,000 and the cleaning up bill £30,000. It failed to mention by way of comparison that the world's military expenditure amounts to over $1,000,000 a minute. In any case, CND had organized teams of cleaners to tidy up during and after the demonstration.

The *Daily Mail* dubbed the demonstration 'unilateralist' – a term which has been frequently used by the government to counter cruise missile protest. The government and the media often try to give the impression that the whole peace movement wants complete and immediate 'one-sided' disarmament by Britain alone, whereas the majority probably favour a freeze and unilateral reductions. The nuclear issue is often portrayed in black and white 'all or nothing' terms to raise public support for the official policy – a policy which encourages escalation.

The *Daily Star* carried the 'exclusive' front page headline: 'Spies Alert Over Peace Army'. The paper implied a connection between the peace movement and three Soviet officials who had been expelled from Britain the previous day. The *Star* quoted a member of the Conservative party saying that 'we must always be alert to the *possibility* of the Soviet government meddling in these waters. Their interests are very well served by CND' (our italics). The question which quite obviously could have been asked is whether the expulsions were timed to coincide with the CND demonstration, much as Michael Heseltine's visit to the Berlin Wall was arranged as a counter publicity stunt.

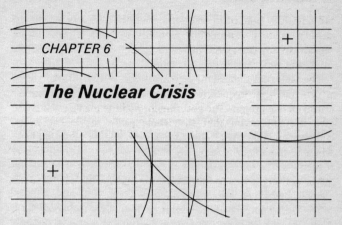

# CHAPTER 6

# *The Nuclear Crisis*

From the preceding chapters it is clear that the nuclear arms race has taken a new and dangerous turn. The swift escalation not only in the numbers but in the capability of the weapons themselves may soon force the adoption of 'launch-on-warning' policies. Nuclear war could break out in less than ten minutes by *accident*. Current NATO strategy is for first use of nuclear weapons such as Cruise or Pershing II in a 'flexible response', leading to limited nuclear war. We argue, in accordance with many military strategists, that such a war, however started, could *not* be limited and would engulf the countries of the northern hemisphere in a war of almost unimaginable proportions. The consequences would be very severe. It is hard to estimate the damage and the death tolls because there are so many uncertainties, but one thing is certain: it would be an unparallelled catastrophe. A recent study[1] of the possible global consequences of nuclear war estimated that out of the total world population of about 4,300,000,000 people, about 138,000,000 people would die from the effects of fire and burns, 916,000,000 from blast and 510,000,000 from the short-term effects of radiation. In addition, about 1,000,000,000 people would be injured by blast or fire, or suffer radiation sickness. In the longer term, as radioactive fall-out spread around the world, about 100,000,000 would die from radiation induced cancers and 50,000,000 suffer severe genetic disorders. The chain-effects of the collapse of the world monetary, economic and distributions systems combined with the pollution of the air and water, and decimation of flora and fauna would mean that hundreds of millions of people in the Third World countries, largely in the southern hemisphere, could die from starvation.[2] In the worst case the damage to the earth's protective ozone layer combined with the effects of forest fires and radiation damage could lead to the complete disruption of the earth's ecosystem. Many plants and animals would be killed and the survival of the human race itself would be in doubt.

For the first time in its history not only the human race, but all living things on our planet, may be threatened with extinction. A crisis brought about by man alone. The consequences of nuclear war are so far reaching, because of the highly complex and inter-related nature of the world's social, economic and political systems, that they force us to think in more global terms. There is really no way that one can envisage a nuclear war as something happening 'over there' – it would affect everybody, whether they were directly targeted or not. Even if we take the most optimistic view, that of the human race surviving, we are still talking about the destruction of civilization in the First World countries. In the Third World countries immense suffering and deaths would be caused by the collapse of the world economic system. In the longer term, however, the surviving remnants of the largely rural populations of the undeveloped countries would be the best fitted for survival, relying as they do largely on growing their own food locally. So should it not be the end of the human race, one might envisage a new world system emerging with the former Third World countries as major world powers. But what legacy of power would they inherit? Unless the structures which lead to nuclear war had been changed they would eventually suffer another devastating nuclear war.

This is not, however, to say that should there be no threat of nuclear war there would be no world problems. Taking a broad view of the planet upon which we live, the nuclear arms race is the most serious of many indications that as a species we are in a state of crisis. Human beings are now consuming materials and energy as never before and are, as a result, experiencing the problems of increasingly scarce resources and growing economic chaos. We are also destroying and polluting our environment at an alarming rate.

The consequences of these factors are severe. Every week about 300,000 people die of starvation, a death toll equivalent to two Hiroshimas every week – equivalent to a continuing nuclear war on our very own doorsteps. Alongside this, the ever widening gap between the riches of the First World countries and the poverty of the Third World countries is considered to be one of the most fundamental threats to long-term world peace.[3] World spending on conventional arms is also rising sharply along with dramatic developments in these weapons' ability to kill large numbers of people. Weapons such as the cluster bomb, which explodes in the air and showers shrapnel over a wide area, are capable of widespread and indiscriminate killing of both military personnel and civilian populations. Some modern conventional weapons are also comparable in their destructive power to the smaller atomic weapons. An example of such a 'quasi-nuclear' weapon is the Fuel Air Explosive, used towards the end of the Vietnam War and known as the 'Daisy Cutter' BLU 82/B. A mixture of highly explosive gases is dispersed in a cloud over the target, and is then ignited, producing a powerful blast wave, capable of razing houses to the ground over a wide area. This weapon has been described as 'the explosive most comparable to a nuclear bomb'.[4] Such developments in the technology of killing people have contributed to the death toll of tens of millions of people who have died in various 'local' wars since the Second World War.

## The causes of the arms race

If we consider the world as a unit, the nuclear arms race can be viewed as one of the most threatening aspects of an overall crisis but cannot be viewed in isolation from it. For example, it is often stated that there are very strong links between the world economic system and the arms race. It might however be more correct to say that world arms spending, currently at over $650,000,000,000 a year, *is* a substantial part of the world economy. As such, spending on arms is a major sector in most countries' economies, taking as much as ten per cent of the Gross National Products of NATO, the Warsaw Pact countries and the People's Republic of China. In the United States the average family pays more in taxes to support the arms race than to educate their children, while developing countries use roughly five times more foreign exchange for arms imports than for agricultural machinery.[5]

The United States and the Soviet Union account for roughly two thirds of the weapons exported to other nations with the Middle East the biggest customer. The United States exported 34 per cent of the arms sold abroad and the Soviet Union 37 per cent. France accounts for 10 per cent, while Italy, the UK and West Germany come rather further behind with 11 per cent between them.[6]

Because of such high levels of spending, the international arms trade is very big business. Multinational corporations are thus heavily involved, directly or indirectly. Lockheed and Northrop are the two main companies handling the bulk of military spending in the USA, but companies such as Exxon, General Motors and ITT are involved in over $50,000,000,000 worth of global sales.[7] This is a stupendous level of spending considered in the light of the fact that *most countries in the world* have a national income or Gross National Product less than this. The USA, USSR, India, China, Brazil and most of the countries in Europe are the only countries which have national incomes of over this level. If money represents power, the top trans-national corporations have an influence greater than most of the countries in the United Nations, an influence which is not and indeed cannot be checked by controls operating at a national level.[8] Such influence is also not checked by the ballot box, but influenced largely by shareholders whose primary goal is profit. Such arguments lead some people to argue that the multinationals control or lead the arms race.

The Technical Marketing Society of America and the Technology Transfer Society, organizations formed 'largely out of the need to convert the inventory of defense, space, and energy research and development into benefits for all mankind', give the impression that the arms manufacturers attempt to lead the military towards buying the new weapons they have developed. Their glossy leaflets advertise seminars on such topics as 'Equipping the Battlefield – Market Opportunities' and 'How Can Industry Help Define NATO Requirements?'[9] This brings us to another conventional cause ascribed to the arms race: science and technology. Over 40 per cent of the world's scientists and technologists are working on some aspect of arms or arms-related development. The new weapons all rely more and more heavily upon ever increasing levels of sophisticated technology. Without the scientists, engineers and technologists, the arms race would not exist. Scientists have in fact been involved with arms development since wars were first fought between 'civilized' societies. Zuckerman[10] argues that scientists lead the arms race by continually inventing new weapons which make the old ones appear obsolete. In conventional economic terms, the scientists provide the ideal consumer product – one in which the profit margins are high, in which cost escalation is taken for granted and rarely incurs penalties, and one which rapidly becomes 'obsolete'. Yet just such an 'ideal product', viewed from a short-term economic perspective, may have built into itself the very seeds of its own destruction. A comparison of countries' spending on arms with industrial output shows a clear link between arms spending and lack of industrial growth.[5] This may be because diverting substantial capital away from the civilian sector impedes long-term growth. This is not surprising as weapons are hardly socially useful products which can be purchased by the civilian consumer. To quote Adam Smith in *The Wealth of Nations*: 'The whole army and navy are unproductive labourers. They are the servants of the public, and are maintained by a part of the annual produce of the industry of other people. Their service, how honourable, how useful, or how necessary soever, produces nothing for which an equal quantity of services can afterwards be procured.' It should also be remembered that equivalent spending on non-military projects creates far more employment than on military ones.

High military expenditure can cause inflation in several ways. Firstly, military expenditure creates a demand without any off-setting increase in consumable output; this excess demand then creates an upward pressure on prices throughout the economy. Secondly, military costs are themselves extremely inflationary because of their highly capital- and technology-intensive nature. These costs are then passed on to the consumer and we pay for them in increased taxes.

The military and the politicians who actually buy the weapons are another key element in the complex industrial, scientific and economic factors fuelling the arms race. The arms race would certainly collapse without their cooperation, doubly so, because in many cases both the military and the politicians hold positions on the boards of the companies actually manufacturing the weapons. In such cases their cooperation is quite complicit. The military attitude can be held responsible for the arms race, because for their own side's safety they always want to be ahead of their opponent or opponents combined; thus escalation proceeds as each side attempts to overtake the other. Both politicians and the military may also wish to possess more nuclear weapons as concrete representations of personal or national power.

It is worth considering a somewhat more radical perspective. It is overwhelmingly men who build, buy and sell, and intend to use nuclear weapons and, from this masculine perspective, the weapons become powerful symbols of a nation's potency. Brian Easlea, in his book *Fathering the Unthinkable*, shows that much of the jargon and imagery associated with the atomic bomb has a remarkably sexual basis. For example, it was decided to call the result of the first atomic test a 'boy' if it worked and produced a massive explosion, but a 'girl' if it fizzled out. He concludes: 'it is my opinion, then, that the principal driving force of the nuclear arms race is ... masculine motivation – in essence, the compulsive desire to lord it over other people and non-human nature, and then manfully to confront a dangerous world'.[11] A placard seen at the June 1982 CND demonstration in London with a picture of a cruise missile rather sums up this idea with the slogan: 'Take the toys away from the boys'. This viewpoint is shared by many of the women of the Women's Peace Camp at Greenham Common, and is one of the reasons for their women-only rule.

## An underlying cause?

So, considering the arms race as a whole, the multi- and transnational corporations, the scientists, masculine attitudes, the military and the politicians can all be seen to have key roles. Furthermore, all these constituents of the arms race play out their roles in a game where short-term gains are sought by individuals, nations, or corporations at the expense of other players. The game is highly competitive and the stakes are high. Long-term, global or moral considerations are not applied. Some people refer to this as the military–industrial complex and thus assign blame collectively, while others single out particular economic, social, political or geographic factors as being more at fault. All these analyses have their own perfectly valid perspectives, but do not take a broad enough view of all the issues concerned.

Of course, within their own environment, all the individuals who collectively add up to, and can be identified as, the military–industrial complex can justify their positions in apparently very sane and rational ways. The big corporations can justify their position by stating how many people they give jobs to who rely on them making a profit, and how their work is for the national defence. The scientists employed on the projects can also state that they are working for the defence of their country, or alternatively that they are just very interested in the scientific aspects and do not take any of the decisions anyway. The military will state that they have to keep up with, or preferably ahead of, the other side. The politicians state that it is their duty to maintain the security of the people they govern and who demand weapons to defend them against 'the Russians' or a re-emergent re-armed Germany in the case of the USSR.

All these justifications, and there are many others, only make sense in terms of a viewpoint of the world which is centred on the individual or on a particular group to the exclusion of everyone else, and which operates purely for the short-term gain of that individual or group – an essentially egocentric viewpoint.

A simple example of this operating at a personal level is the opposing positions people take in argument. Two people with fundamentally different viewpoints will construct quite logical, but of course quite contradictory, arguments based on their different beliefs or drives. Any discussions they have, unless these fundamental viewpoints change, can only reinforce their positions. Thus, their views become more and more polarized.

A similar mechanism can operate at a national level where the consequences are likely to be more severe. The formation of the policy of deterrence, for example, is designed, at least in part, to produce a particular effect in the minds of our supposed opponent. So, in this country, a key factor in deciding our policy is what effect *we* think our policies have on Warsaw Pact thinking. But we can only form an opinion on what the Warsaw Pact countries believe through the filter of our own belief system. In fact, what we think that they are thinking is most likely to reflect only our own prejudices. Our notion of our opponent is thus little more than an almost perfect mirror of our own beliefs and prejudices, and the same can be said of their view of us.

Our view of our opponent is very important when we come to consider why the Soviet Union and the United States do not see eye to eye and why arms negotiations have failed so dismally. Some insight into the minds of the US and Soviet spokesmen can be seen in the following statements made by President Reagan of the USA and the late President Brezhnev of the Soviet Union. In Florida on 8 March 1983, President Reagan accused the Soviets of having 'the aggressive impulses of an evil empire' and said of the United States, 'We will never compromise our principles and standards ... let us be aware that while they [the USSR] preach the supremacy of the state, declare its omnipotence over individual man and predict its eventual domination of all people, they are the focus of evil in the modern world' (*Guardian*, 9 March 1983). In other words, we (the USA) are right and good, and they (the USSR) are wrong and evil.

In a similar way, but from a completely opposite viewpoint, Brezhnev stated: 'The impression is increasingly being formed in the world of the United States as an absolutely unreliable partner in inter-state ties, as a state whose leadership, prompted by some whim, caprice or emotional outburst, or by considerations of narrowly understood immediate advantage, is capable at any moment of violating its international obligations and cancelling treaties and agreements signed by it. There is hardly any need to explain what a dangerous destabilizing impact this has on the entire international situation ...' (*Soviet News*, 12 January 1980).

Certainly the starting point for such statements did not come from a cool, rational appraisal of the state of the world. Both sides are poles apart and speaking from entrenched positions of mutual mistrust and fear. The only way out of this apparent deadlock is for one or both sides to modify their perceptions of the other and to take action to build up trust between them.

To some extent both sides are their own worst enemy because in this emotionally charged rhetoric the 'evil' or 'capricious' enemy in many ways exists only as long as a belief in it does.

## Who is responsible?

So where does the responsibility lie? With the military, the politicians, big business, the scientists, nationalism or somewhere else? In reality it lies with *all of them* and *all of us*. Essentially one cannot divorce oneself completely from all these conventionally blamed causes. Nearly all of us in many, though maybe very small, ways are fuelling them. But a lot of people doing a little adds up to a lot of support. Collectively we are certainly responsible for the systems which have created and which support the arms race, world starvation and all the rest. *Individually* we are all responsible whether we *actively* support them or not. By our very silence we endorse the existing world systems. It is no more a political act to actively oppose an issue than it is to remain silent. Silence is active endorsement.

Currently the catastrophe of nuclear war is discussed largely in national terms. The global issues are seldom discussed and the influence of purely personal or local issues seems to have been lost.

Once we realize that perceptions are central to the issue, we can then shift our viewpoint to encompass both the global and the personal issues. The global issues are then understood to be mirroring our own personal internal beliefs. This point of view is central when we come to consider what can be done and what we as individuals can do.

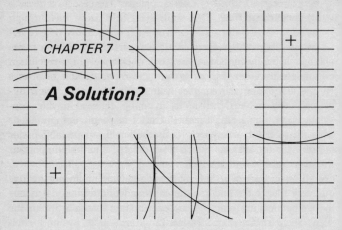

# CHAPTER 7

# A Solution?

The most important short-term priority is to reduce the growing risk of nuclear war. There are many ways of achieving this, but all require initiative and commitment by individuals and governments alike.

A modest but significant first step towards establishing mutual trust is for various countries from both East and West alliances to act individually, or in concert, to voluntarily reduce their nuclear arsenals by some small amount. Such a gesture would hardly reduce the 'overkill capacity' but would at least help to diminish the wall of fear engulfing our planet.

The way to instil trust is by gradual steps whose progress is predictable, observable and readily achieved. In this respect the so-called zero option and the Soviet counter-proposals both fail – they ask for bold steps to be taken in a propagandized arena, rampant with suspicion and fear, and devoid of any trust.

There have been a number of major international proposals for greater security which the British government should support unconditionally. These proposals, some of which are discussed elsewhere, are briefly listed below. None of them would reduce our security. Most would improve it.

1. An immediate bilateral nuclear weapons freeze, prohibiting the testing, production and deployment of all new missiles and all

new aircraft which carry nuclear bombs.[1] The case for a freeze is overwhelming. The USA and the USSR now have rough weapons parity and could destroy each other many times over; continuation of the arms race endangers us all. Such a freeze could be easily verified by satellite surveillance – high resolution satellite photography can give a clear photograph of objects one foot across viewed from a height of 100 miles.[2] New aircraft and nuclear submarines can be detected during construction. Shipyards, aircraft factories and runways cannot be hidden. New missile silos can also be readily spotted. No major infringement of a treaty could evade detection (with the important exception of cruise missiles).

2. The setting up of an International Satellite Monitoring Agency under UN control to provide an independent international means of treaty verification.[3] This idea was first put forward to the UN at the first special session on disarmament by the French government in 1978. Since then the superpowers have shown little interest.

3. A comprehensive nuclear test ban treaty to prohibit all nuclear testing (above and below ground). This would prevent the production of new types of warhead and would be a significant step in halting the arms race. Satellites can check for above ground explosions, while below ground explosions can be verified by sensitive ground shock monitors (seismographs).

4. The establishment of a battlefield-nuclear-weapon-free zone in Europe as recommended by the Independent Commission on Disarmament and Security Issues.[4] Initially the zone should be extended 150 km either side of the East–West border. It would prevent the early use of tactical nuclear weapons in any conflict. Eventually the zone should be widened. In addition, no new tactical 'mini-nukes', such as neutron bombs, should be based in Europe.

5. An immediate ban on all weapons in outer space. The 1967 Outer Space Treaty only banned weapons of mass destruction and did not forbid either anti-satellite weapons or anti-ballistic missile 'beam' weapons for deployment in outer space (see Appendix 2). Developments in beam weapon technology mean that there may shortly be a new arms race in space.

This must be stopped before it ever gets off the ground. A Soviet proposal in 1981 to extend the 1967 treaty to include all weapons in space should be agreed upon immediately.

6. A ban on the production of high-grade fissionable nuclear material for weapons.[5] This would help limit the world's nuclear arsenals at their present levels and stem the spread of weapons to other countries. It would be verifiable under the International Atomic Energy Authority's fuel cycle 'safeguard' system. (They make reactor inspections internationally and could identify all significant infringements.)

7. A worldwide halt on weapons research and development, combined with extensive research programmes on the conversion of military expenditure and procurement efforts into peaceful applications. Such conversion schemes would have a major impact on reducing world inflation and unemployment. This can only be achieved by greater awareness amongst the scientific community and by more emphasis on social responsibility in science education in schools and universities.

In addition, the British government should, as a first step, renounce cruise and Trident missiles which, as we have seen, represent a gross escalation in nuclear weaponry. Furthermore, misleading nuclear propaganda should be immediately withdrawn – publications such as the Ministry of Defence leaflets 'Cruise Missiles – A Vital Part of the West's Life Insurance', and 'How to Deal with a Bully', the Foreign Office wall-chart 'Arms Control and Disarmament', and the government films 'A Better Road to Peace' and 'The Peace Game'. These last four – propaganda aimed at schoolchildren – are particularly dangerous because not only do they fail to give an accurate representation of the real global nuclear picture, but they also perpetuate that sense of mistrust and fear which has kept the arms race going for so long. The departments producing this material should clearly be more publicly accountable.

Above all we are compelled to ask the question: Why, if the government's case for new nuclear weapons is so strong, has it become necessary to disseminate this inaccurate and highly distorted propaganda to justify it?

## Taking action

None of the objectives listed above can be realized without the political will to achieve them, and substantial shifts in attitudes are needed before any such proposals will appear workable and acceptable to all parties.

But if, as described before, the underlying problem is essentially one of our perception, as a result of which everyone is responsible for the fear and mistrust which drives the arms race, the way forward starts to become clear. These apparently intangible and global issues transform themselves into very real personal ones – well within an individual's sphere of action.

An essential basis for action is the belief that human beings do not, by nature, desire to kill each other, and that the forces which have operated in the past, causing people to do just that, do not need to form an unavoidable and repeating pattern for the future.

Many societies, supposedly more primitive than ours, have developed in ways which are inherently peaceful and stable. Of course, they have never developed nuclear weapons and in some cases have not 'progressed' – if this is the correct word – from very simple levels of technology. It is indeed ironical that it is as a result of our very own 'progress' that we may halt our development as a species for good.

Essentially all of us at present exist in a context where nuclear war can 'happen', and may happen sooner rather than later. All of us create this present context. It follows then that we could create a new context in which nuclear war is not inevitable, indeed, one in which it could not occur. Everything could then be viewed in terms of bringing about world peace or getting rid of nuclear weapons and not in terms of struggling against nuclear weapons. As far as action is concerned, it is vital to realize that *not* doing is also very important. All those who at present 'do' nothing are in fact making a powerful statement too. In their non-action they are supporting and accepting the way things are now, the status quo. What this means is that *all* actions are important and that it is only your level of awareness of world problems which limits your ability to affect them. In this sense all of us are at the sharp end of the peace movement.

Action can be viewed at three levels: global, local and personal. Most 'conventional' peace movements operate in a local and global sense, motivated in some part by fear of the nuclear weapons. The influence of the individual and the possible effects of personal direct action are commonly overlooked.

The term 'direct action' spans a whole spectrum of possibilities from writing a letter, marching in a demonstration, to civil disobedience or engaging in terrorist activity. Obviously each individual has to make his or her own decision about how far to go for an ideal or cause and which sort of action is appropriate. To some the advent of nuclear war may appear such an immediate threat that they feel that any actions which stop it are justified. But it is absolutely vital only to take action which is completely consistent with the sort of world you wish to create and live in. We do not believe that peace can ultimately be achieved through violence. This may be possible in the shorter term, but in the longer term, because the root cause of the problem will not have been tackled, the issue will eventually re-emerge.

We shall therefore concentrate on non-violent direct action or non-cooperation. The practical basis of non-cooperation is simple: no individual is an island. There is scarcely anything we do, or refrain from doing, that does not affect or depend on other people. Yet the way everybody depends on everybody else is so pervasive that we take it largely for granted and seldom stop to think about it or realize its profound political implications. As Martin Luther King Jr said: 'It really boils down to this: that all life is interrelated. We are all caught in an inescapable network of mutuality, tied into a single garment of destiny. Whatever affects one directly, affects all indirectly. We are made to live together because of the inter-related structure of reality.'[6] As the world population increases and more and more people live in towns and cities, and as we become more socially organized and dependent upon technology, the world is growing effectively smaller because of modern means of transport and communication. In this process we are all becoming less isolated and more dependent on each other.

This dependence increases the practical potential of non-cooperation. The non-violent activist can use this potential base of power by withholding cooperation from what is seen as evil or unacceptable and actively supporting that which is seen as good. But in order to deal effectively with institutionalized evils, individuals must organize. While an individual can act effectively to spread information, an organization can exert coercive power. It was this development of organized group and mass non-violent action such as strikes and boycotts which was the key to Gandhi's successes in India.

Yet even an individual act of non-cooperation can work as a catalyst to break the ice of hopelessness and apathy. Thoreau wrote in 1866 (of civil disobedience as a means to defeat slavery): 'If one *honest* man, in the state of Massachusetts, *ceasing to hold slaves*, were actually to withdraw from this copartnership, and be locked up in the county jail therefore, it would be the abolition of slavery in America. For it matters not how small the beginning may seem to be: what is once well done is done forever.'[7] In this way one person's action acts as an example to many who, while they may be seething over an injustice, either do not see what they could do, feel an illusory isolation or hesitate to act out of fear. Refusal to cooperate, if the climate for change is right, can then spread in an almost infectious manner. But first the climate for change must be created. To paraphrase Victor Hugo, 'all the forces in the world are not so powerful as an idea whose time has come'. The first part of the task therefore is to create just such a climate.

## Our choice

The nuclear arms issue is inextricably bound up in a web of interrelated world problems. Ultimate and lasting change can only come through radical changes in perspectives, perceptions and interactions of people on a very individual level which will occur hand in hand with the reorganization of society and nations on a local and global scale.

Despite the need for this global shift in perception any such shift will only arise as the result of individuals changing their point of view. We argue that the fundamental process for change is a personal one and that the fundamental cause of our crisis is both a collective and an individual one. Once enough individuals have changed, we may see a reaction in society rather like the chain reaction in an atomic bomb when the 'critical mass' is reached, only in this case the critical mass for a revolutionary change of a non-destructive nature would have occurred before the weapons themselves were detonated. The effect of one person influencing five others and they in turn five more reaches 50,000,000 people in eleven steps – about the population of this country!

From our own personal viewpoints we feel that we either adapt as a species or die in our own man-made catastrophe. We thus make a heartfelt plea for a shift in perception to encompass both the global and personal aspects of our predicament, enabling us all to have a future, as humanity, for humanity, on our one Earth.

As individuals or groups we exercise power whether we act or not. We can change. Nuclear war is not inevitable. The abolition of cruise missiles will be just the beginning.

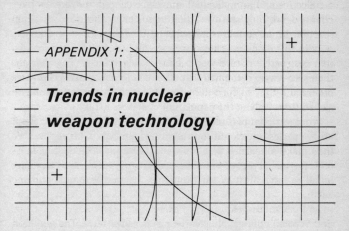

# Trends in nuclear weapon technology

The first nuclear bombs (known as A-bombs) worked on the principle of nuclear fission. The radioactive nuclei of fissionable material such as uranium 235 and plutonium 239 have a tendency to spontaneously break up, emitting neutrons and generating heat. The neutrons emitted by one such radioactive disintegration can cause other nuclei to follow suit. If the lump of fissionable material exceeds a certain 'critical' mass (a few kilograms for uranium 235) the radioactive disintegration results in an explosive chain reaction as one disintegrating nucleus induces others to disintegrate, and they in turn induce others. The chain reaction takes place within a fraction of a second and the enormous amounts of energy released in the form of heat, blast, and radiation are exceptionally destructive, as was proved by the attacks on Hiroshima and Nagasaki.

A-bombs are limited to an explosive power in the kiloton range. The second generation of nuclear bombs (the H-bombs) which use nuclear fusion were first tested in 1952 by the United States. It was found that the nuclei of light atoms such as hydrogen could be induced to fuse together yielding vast quantities of energy and generating even more massive explosions than fission devices. The most powerful nuclear bomb ever tested was a fusion device and had an explosive power of 60 megatons (equivalent to sixty million tons of TNT) which is capable of totally devastating an area thirty miles in diameter. No bombs of this power, however, are currently deployed as weapons. Current nuclear warheads have explosive yields ranging from less than 1 kiloton (so-called 'battlefield' nuclear weapons) up to 10 megatons (e.g. the US Titan-II and the Soviet SS-18).[1] Fission bombs are detonated by using high explosive to force two sub-critical masses of fissionable material together to create an explosive super-critical mass. Fusion weapons are detonated by a fission bomb trigger which generates the high temperatures necessary for the fusion reactions to take place. Many modern weapons are three stage 'fission-fusion-fission' devices. The bomb casings include neutron reflecting materials to accelerate the chain reactions and generate the maximum explosive force. It is worth noting, contrary to the beliefs of many people, that nuclear warheads can be dismantled as easily as they can be manufactured. Once constructed there is nothing 'magical' about them which prevents their disposal.

The radius of destruction for a given warhead depends on the cube root of its explosive yield. On account of this a ten-fold increase in explosive power increases the area of destruction by a factor of 4.64. For this reason it is more efficient (in terms of both the amount of scarce nuclear material and the extent of destruction) to use several small warheads to attack a target than one very powerful warhead. Most warheads in strategic nuclear forces are therefore less than a megaton in size. Considerable increases in the accuracy of delivery systems over the last few years have meant that warheads smaller than was possible a decade ago can now be assigned to designated targets and still maintain the same destructive potential. The warheads on the Soviet SS-20 missile for example have an explosive yield of 150 kT and the warheads on the ground-launched cruise missiles have a yield of 200 kT.

One of the most significant changes in warhead characteristics since the Second World War has been the rapid increase in 'yield-to-weight ratio' (i.e. the explosive power of the bomb compared with its overall weight). This improvement has been made to get round the problem of weight restriction on missile-borne warheads which have to be carried well above the earth's atmosphere for an intercontinental flight to their targets. It has meant that multiple warheads can now be carried on one launcher. The Hiroshima bomb had a yield-to-weight ratio of about 0.003 kilotons yield per kilogram. The US Poseidon SLBM 40 kT warhead (which weighs 100 kilograms) has a yield-to-weight ratio of 0.4 kilotons yield per kilogram – over a hundred times greater than 'Little Boy'. New warhead construction techniques, minimizing both size and weight, have enabled nuclear artillery shells to be developed which can be fired from 155 mm Howitzers known as 'dual capable', i.e. both conventional high explosive and nuclear tipped shells can be fired. It is now believed, at least of US weapons, that 'this miniaturization of nuclear warheads is now, in some applications, close to the limits set by the laws of physics'.[2] The small size of modern warheads enables them to be carried by small delivery vehicles (such as cruise missiles) which have less chance of being spotted by radar. Miniaturization has also led to the production of nuclear depth-charges for anti-submarine warfare and atomic demolition mines with yields of a few tons.[3]

The other significant development in warhead design has been the introduction of new bomb casings to enhance the radiation effects. The so-called 'neutron bomb' is the prime example of this. The neutron bomb or 'enhanced radiation' (ER) weapon is a 'mini-nuke' tactical weapon intended for use against tank forces. These bombs have comparatively low yield (about 1 kT) but are designed to produce more energetic neutrons than normal warheads by the fusion of deuterium and tritium (forms of heavy hydrogen). At ranges where a tank crew would be safe from heat and blast, the enormous burst of neutrons produced by an ER weapon can easily penetrate conventional tank armour and would provide lethal doses of radiation. The effects of very high doses of neutron radiation (e.g. > 3000 rads) are particularly unpleasant, causing immediate nausea and vomiting followed by loss of control of movement and death within a few days due to failure of breathing or brain damage. A 1 kT ER weapon will give this dose of radiation over 800 m from ground-zero.[4] Heat and blast are not negligible however and would have very damaging effects. Radiation would also not be restricted entirely to the battlefield.

## Means of delivery

From 1945 until the mid-1950s propeller-driven bombers were the only vehicles available for delivering nuclear weapons to their targets. Bombers such as the US B-29s and the Soviet Tu-4 were comparatively slow and of limited capability in waging an intercontinental war. From the mid-1950s, however, jet bombers (such as the US B-52) were developed with intercontinental ranges (about 10,000 miles) which could cruise at sub-sonic speeds carrying weapons loads in excess of thirty tons. The B-52s and the long-range Soviet turbo-prop Mya-4 ('Bison') and Tu-95 ('Bear') bombers provided the mainstay of the strategic nuclear forces until the advent of missile delivery systems.

In 1957, the USSR astonished the world (particularly the United States) by successfully launching a satellite (Sputnik) into a low earth orbit thereby demonstrating the ability to construct rockets capable of carrying nuclear weapons on intercontinental trajectories. Within a few years the first intercontinental ballistic missiles (ICBMs) were deployed by the two superpowers. ICBMs had the distinct advantage over bombers in that they could reach their targets in less than half an hour (a small fraction of the time taken by bomb-carrying jet aircraft). Also, bombers were becoming increasingly vulnerable to improved air defence systems (interceptor aircraft and anti-aircraft missiles). During the 1960s land-based ICBMs were deployed in their hundreds. Submarine-based missiles were also deployed for greater invulnerability. For almost two decades now the USA has relied on the so-called 'strategic triad' weapons in the sea, on the land and in the air – a combined strategic force of B-52 bombers, Minuteman ICBMs, plus Poseidon and Polaris SLBMs (now being replaced by Trident). The USSR has relied mainly on ICBMs and SLBMs. All aspects of these strategic weapons together with the intermediate-range nuclear forces in Europe are now undergoing substantial revision.

Intercontinental missiles have been undergoing gradual development on several fronts. Launchers have been designed with increasing 'throw-weight' (i.e. weight of payload) to enable one rocket to carry several independently targetable warheads on intercontinental trajectories. The US Minuteman III, for example, carries three warheads and has a throw-weight of about 1 ton whereas the MX missile (now under development) has a throw-weight of over 3.5 tons and will be designed to carry at least ten warheads[5] – possibly more if the SALT-2 treaty is not adhered to.

Rockets are also now being converted from 'hot launch' to 'cold launch'. In the hot-launch mode a missile is ignited in the silo and causes substantial damage to the silo which cannot then be re-used. In the new cold-launch mode silo damage is minimized although silos would still be unusable for a few days. The modern Soviet SS-17, SS-18, and SS-19 ICBMs are cold-launch missiles. One further development has been the replacement of old liquid-fuelled missiles with solid-fuelled missiles. Liquid fuel is unstable, requires refrigeration, and precludes mobility.

Missile payloads have steadily increased from the single warhead payloads of the early 1960s to the multiple warheads now in use. Multiple warheads may be of the MRV or MIRV type. The earliest multiple warheads were of the MRV (multiple re-entry vehicle) type. Missiles with MRV shed all of their warheads at the same point in their intercontinental space flight. The warheads then re-enter the earth's atmosphere and fall around the designated target thus providing a 'shower' of nuclear bursts in one locality. Thus only one target can be attacked with MRV. Missiles with MIRV (multiple independently targetable re-entry vehicles) shed their warheads one at a time and change course in between. In this way each warhead may be directed against a different target (see Figure 13). To attack a number of separate ground targets it is much more economical to use large throw-weight launch vehicles, carrying a high number of MIRV warheads, than to use several small missiles carrying fewer warheads. The most up-to-date ICBMs and SLBMs are being designed with this aim in mind. For example, the Soviet SS-18 missile introduced in 1977 carries eight 500 kT MIRV warheads, the US Trident C-4 SLBM introduced in 1979 carries eight 100 kT warheads, and the projected Trident D-5 (like the MX) will carry at least ten 335 kT warheads per launcher. Manoeuvring warheads (MaRV) are now being deployed ostensibly as a means to avoid Soviet anti-ballistic missile defences (ABMs) around Moscow. The Chevaline warheads fitted to the

British Polaris SLBMs are probably of this type.[6] Apart from improvements in missile throw-weight, payloads, and launch mode, the most strategically significant improvements are now being made in missile navigation and accuracy.

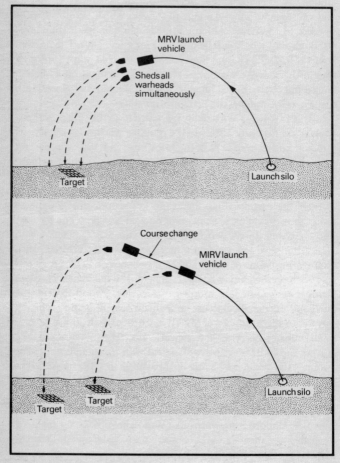

*Figure 13.* MRV and MIRV warheads

## Missile accuracy and navigation

Figure 14 shows the general trends in weapon accuracy over the last two decades and the expected trend into the next. It is quite clear that at all times since the development of the first nuclear missiles the US weapons have had much greater accuracy than the Soviet weapons – this fact is still true today and will continue to be true for some time. The improvements in accuracy have

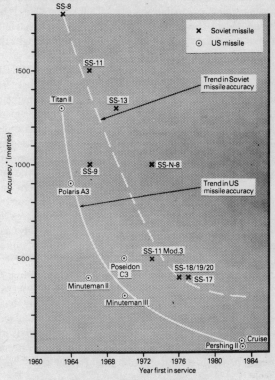

*Figure 14.* Trends in missile accuracy
*The accuracy is the CIRCULAR ERROR PROBABLE – the radius of a circle within which fifty per cent of the missiles would fall

resulted from technological innovations in in-flight and near-target (terminal) guidance.

In-flight navigation for ICBMs and SLBMs is primarily based on inertial guidance systems. Such systems need to know the precise starting point of the flight-path. This is not a difficult problem for land-based ICBMs but is not so easy for SLBMs – consequently SLBMs still do not have as high an accuracy as ICBMs. A recent move by the Americans will shortly revolutionize in-flight navigation for ballistic missiles. A new global positioning system (GPS) based on a network of geostationary NAVSTAR satellites is being established. When the complete network of eighteen satellites is operational it will provide missiles with continuous in-flight three-dimensional position fixes to within ten metres.[7]

For cruise missiles the terrain contour matching (TERCOM) guidance system has been developed.[8] This system uses radar to scan the landscape. The received information is compared with a ground contour 'map' stored in the missile's computer memory (see Figure 15). A further system, the terminal guidance digital scene-matching area correlator (DSMAC), is being developed to supplement TERCOM. The TERCOM system enables cruise missiles to hit their targets to within fifty metres. At the end of 1982 it was reported, however, that the US government had to set up a special team to iron out some problems associated with TERCOM[9] primarily because it could not stop the missiles flying into power cables. Also some snow-covered Arctic terrain has few recognizable features for the missiles to follow on flights into the Soviet Union.

One other terminal guidance system, RADAG (radar area guidance), has been developed for the Pershing II IRBM. RADAG is the most advanced terminal guidance system of any ballistic missile[10] in the w ld and it gives the Pershing II its incredibly high accuracy of a few tens of metres. It is expected that many other ballistic missiles will be equipped with similar terminal guidance systems in the future, MX and Trident D-5 being the most likely.

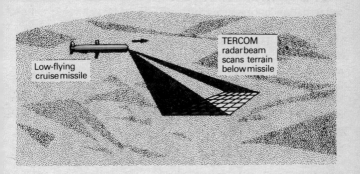

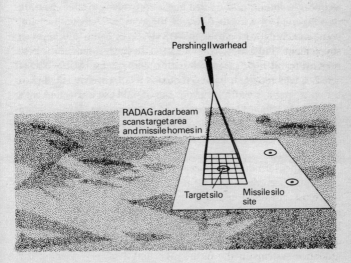

*Figure 15*. Cruise and Pershing II guidance systems

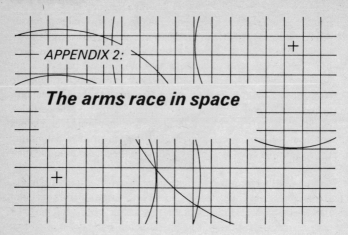

# APPENDIX 2:

# The arms race in space

Orbiting satellites have been used for many years as essential military communication links and as providers of intelligence information about military forces on the ground. These military uses of outer space have been comparatively passive and, until recently, no weapons have been based in space. In the last few years, however, there has been an upsurge in research on a variety of ideas for space-based weapons and weapons related systems, and plans are now being drawn up by both the US and the USSR for basing actual weapons systems in space and not merely guidance, surveillance, or communication support systems.

## Anti-satellite weapons

Both East and West have developed hunter-killer satellites which carry explosive charges. These killer satellites manoeuvre close to their target and then blow up themselves and their target. Such weapons have already been tested and soon no support satellites in space will be safe from attack.

## Beam weapons

The latest and most radical ideas for space-based military systems may result in a complete upset of the present nuclear balance. Some military planners now have visions of placing anti-ballistic missile defence systems in orbit to eradicate the threat posed by ICBMs. Implausible though they seem, several schemes have now been proposed for the use of massive laser beam and particle beam weapons for missile defence – the laser or particle beam 'guns' to be carried on orbiting space stations. The idea is that such weapons, generating high energy beams of radiation or sub-nuclear particles, could attack an ICBM force from above just after launch and knock out the missiles by completely disabling their electronics, detonating their explosive fuses, or burning a hole in their sides to ignite their fuel.

There have been many hypothetical designs for such weapons, some relying on high energy lasers with large mirrors to point the beam towards its target, others using beams of particles accelerated by electric and magnetic fields. Both types of system pose extremely formidable technological problems. It has indeed been suggested that the technology required for such weapons does not yet exist, and that even if it did the ease of producing effective counter-measures renders them useless anyway.[1] Certainly there are serious problems in making such systems work. For example laser beams tend to spread out as they propagate and it would be difficult to concentrate enough energy in the beam to rapidly disable a missile at a range of say 1000 kilometres. Charged particle beams can be deflected and distorted by the earth's magnetic field, rendering them useless too. Also there are major technical difficulties in detecting a target missile to within a metre or so at a range of 1000 kilometres, and directing a beam onto it within the space of a second or two – the only time available if a whole force of several hundred ICBMs is to be destroyed in flight.

The overall impression is that such systems are not technologically feasible at present, though that is not to say that they won't be at some time in the future – after all the atomic bomb was not technically feasible before the Second World War, but a massive research effort soon changed that. This is perhaps why so much funding is now going into secret laser and particle beam technology. What is clear to the outside observer, however, is that even if such weapons are created and made to be effective, the arms race will only go much further. There will be renewed efforts to find alternative forms of warhead delivery and counter-measures, and less reliance will be placed on ballistic missiles (this will favour the US, which has more advanced cruise missile technology than the USSR). There can be no real human benefit in relentlessly pursuing such research, which has the potential to fuel the arms race for decades to come, and to waste human endeavour on purely destructive tasks well into the twenty-first century. Even the superficially innocuous space programme (e.g. the space shuttle) must be viewed with suspicion in the light of the new military plans for the use of outer space. The shuttle makes an ideal vehicle with which to service orbiting weapons platforms. 'The US military is so impressed with the re-usable space shuttle, that it has booked no less than a third of the seventy or so shuttle payloads planned to be put into orbit by 1988.'[2]

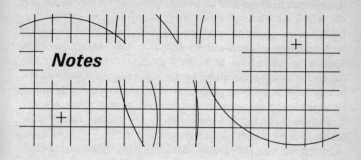

# Notes

## Notes to Chapter 1

1. O. Greene, B. Rubin, N. Turok, P. Webber and G. Wilkinson, *London After the Bomb*, Oxford University Press, Oxford, 1982.

2. British Medical Association (Board of Science and Education), *The Medical Effects of Nuclear War*, John Wiley, Chichester, 1983. See also E. Chivian, S. Chivian, R. J. Lifton and J. E. Mack (eds.), *Last Aid – The Medical Dimensions of Nuclear War*, W. H. Freeman, San Francisco, 1982.

3. Quoted in J. K. Galbraith, *The Age of Uncertainty*, BBC Publications/André Deutsch, London, 1977, (p. 342).

4. *Nuclear Weapons – Report of the UN Secretary General*, Autumn Press, Brookline, Mass., 1980, (p. 8).

5. 'The Strangelove HQ under MAD Mountain', *Observer*, 7 September 1980.

6. Paul Warnke (former Head of US Arms Control Agency), quoted in J. A. Joyce, *The War Machine*, Hamlyn, London, 1981, (pp. 147–8).

7. The Brandt Commission, *Common Crisis*, Pan Books, London, 1983, (p. 37).

8. The Independent Commission on Security and Disarmament Issues, *Common Security – A Programme for Disarmament*, Pan Books, London, 1982, (pp. 71–99).

9. 'Majority disapprove of Britain accepting cruise', *Guardian*, 24 January 1983.

**Notes to Chapter 2**

1. E. Ishikawa and D. L. Swain (eds.), *Hiroshima and Nagasaki – The Physical, Medical and Social Effects of the Atomic Bombings*, Hutchinson, London, 1981.
2. O. Hahn and F. Strassmann, *Die Naturwissenschaften*, vol. 27, 1939, (p. 11).
3. From General Groves's testimony at Robert Oppenheimer's security hearings in 1954, quoted in B. Easlea, *Fathering the Unthinkable*, Pluto Press, London, 1983, (p. 98).
4. J. G. Crowther, *Fifty Years with Science*, Barrie & Jenkins, London, 1970, (p. 259).
5. From the report to President Truman on the Trinity Test, quoted in N. Humphrey, 'The Psychology of the Bomb', *Listener*, 29 October 1981.
6. Quoted by H. York and A. Greb, 'Scientists as Advisers to Governments', in J. Rotblat (ed.), *Scientists, the Arms Race, and Disarmament*, Taylor & Francis/UNESCO, London, 1982, (p. 86).
7. Stockholm International Peace Research Institute, *The Arms Race and Arms Control*, Taylor & Francis, London, 1982.
8. F. Barnaby, 'The Effects of a Global Nuclear War: The Arsenals', *Ambio* (Journal of the Royal Swedish Academy of Sciences), vol. 11, no. 2–3, 1982, (p. 76).
9. R. Forsberg, 'A Bilateral Nuclear-Weapon Freeze', *Scientific American*, vol. 247, November 1982, (pp. 32–41).
10. US Department of Defense, *Report of Secretary Harold Brown to Congress – Fiscal Year 1980*, US Government Printing Office, Washington D.C., 1979, (pp. 8–9).


**Notes to Chapter 3**

1. E. Beard, *Developing the ICBM: A Study in Bureaucratic Politics*, Columbia University Press, New York, 1976, (p. 224).
2. 'Cruise missiles ready to go', *Observer*, 19 December 1982.
3. 'US: New tactical cruise missile', *Defence and Foreign Affairs Daily*, 14 April 1980.
4. R. K. Betts (ed.), *Cruise Missiles: Technology, Strategy, Politics*, Brookings Institution, Washington D.C., 1981, (p. 586).

5. 'Massive Order for Pershing', *Observer*, 13 February 1983.

6. Stockholm International Peace Research Institute, *The Arms Race and Arms Control*, Taylor & Francis, London, 1982, (p. 147).

7. K. Tsipis, 'Cruise Missiles', *Scientific American*, vol. 236, February 1977, (pp. 20–29).

8. N. F. Astbury, H. W. H. West, H. R. Hodgkinson, P. A. Cubbage and R. Clare, 'Gas Explosions in Load Bearing Brick Structures', *British Ceramics Research Association Special Publication* no. 68, 1970.

9. 'Canadian Cruise Test raises Storm among Opposition', *Guardian*, 25 January 1983.

10. 'Fight against Cruise Gets Tough and Rough', *Sanity*, January 1983, (pp. 14–15).

11. 'Cruise Speed-Up Sought by US', *Observer*, 19 December 1982.

12. M. Hewish, 'Countdown to the Cruise', *New Scientist*, 31 March 1983, (pp. 878–83).

13. B. Kent, 'Where the Mafia Waits for the Missiles', *Sanity*, November 1982, (p. 15).

14. US Department of Defense Appropriations for 1983, *Hearings before a Sub-committee of the Committee on Appropriations, House of Representatives, 97th Congress Second Session, Part 4, 1 April 1982*, US Government Printing Office, Washington D.C., 1982, (pp. 400–401).

15. 'Tiger Team keeps Missiles on Target', *Observer*, 21 November 1982.

16. 'Playing Nuclear Poker', *Time Magazine*, 31 January 1983.

17. 'Soviet Traditions that gave Birth to the SS-20', *Observer*, 30 January 1983.

18. 'The MXture as before', *Guardian*, 16 April 1983.

19. 'MX Commission gets more time', *Guardian*, 10 February 1983.

20. D. Gold, C. Paine and G. Shields, *Misguided Expenditure: An Analysis of the Proposed MX Missile System*, Council on Economic Priorities, New York, 1981, (p. 118).

21. 'The General with a Missile Plan to Sell', *Sunday Times*, 10 April 1983.

22. 'The US Off-Target on Soviet Missiles', *Guardian*, 1 March 1983.

## Notes to Chapter 4

1. NATO, Nuclear Planning Group Communiqué, 18 November 1976; Communiqué of the Atlantic Council, 8 December 1976.
2. *Interim Report of the Special Committee on Nuclear Weapons in Europe*, presented by J. Cartwright (SDP) and J. Critchley (Conservative), co-rapporteurs North Atlantic Assembly International Secretariat, November 1982.
3. Quoted by Sir Martin Ryle in 'The Strange Birth of the New Missiles', *Observer*, 6 March 1983.
4. 'How Britain lost veto on US bomb', *Guardian*, 22 February 1983.
5. 'Dual key control "myth" Pentagon man reiterates', *Guardian*, 24 February 1983.
6. 'Heseltine asked to explain dual key', *Guardian*, 15 February 1983.
7. K. Tsipis, 'Cruise missiles', *Scientific American*, vol. 236, February 1977, (p. 20–29).
8. 'Ustinov in New Missile Warning', *Guardian*, 7 April 1983.
9. H. Jackson, 'Cruise missiles obsolete already', *Guardian*, 17 February 1983.
10. Written answers to questions (Defence), *Hansard*, vol. 203, 6 March 1981.
11. *US Dept. of Defense, Annual Report, Fiscal Year 1980*, US Government Printing Office, Washington D.C., January 1979, (p. 148).
12. 'HMS Sheffield thought Exocet was friendly', *New Scientist*, 10 February 1983, (p. 353).
13. SIPRI, *The arms race and arms control*, Taylor & Francis, London, 1982, (p. 144). United Nations, *Nuclear weapons – report of the UN Secretary General*, Autumn Press, Brookline, Massachusetts, 1980, (pp. 213–18).
14. Interviewed in 'The War About Peace' ITV 21 April 1983.
15. United Nations, *Nuclear weapons – report of the UN Secretary General*, Autumn Press, Brookline, Massachusetts, 1980, (pp. 81–2).
16. 'Louis Mountbatten 1979/80: A military commander surveys the nuclear arms race', *International Security*, vol. 4, no. 3, 1980, (pp. 3–5).

17. A critique of the fallacious arguments used in comparing the military forces of East and West is given in: *The nuclear numbers game*, Radical statistics nuclear disarmament group, London, 1982.

18. *Common security – a programme for disarmament*, The Report of the Independent Commission on Disarmament and Security Issues under the chairmanship of Olof Palme, Pan Books, London, 1982, (p. 147).

19. Field Marshal Lord Carver, *A policy for peace*, Faber & Faber, London, 1982, (p. 109).

## Notes to Chapter 5

1. 'The Black and White Missile Show', *Observer*, 2 January 1983.

2. R. Forsberg, 'A Bilateral Nuclear-Weapon Freeze', *Scientific American*, vol. 247, November 1982, (p. 32).

3. 'The KGB's secret war', *Reader's Digest Magazine*, November 1982, (p. 159).

4. 'Soviet peace group faces a bleak winter', *Guardian*, 27 November 1982.

5. 'Heseltine unit set up to fight CND influence' *Guardian*, 2 March 1983.

6. 'The roots of Tory smear against CND', *Observer*, 8 May 1983.

7. C. Aubrey (ed.), *Nukespeak: The Media and the Bomb*, Comedia Publishing Group, London, 1982.

8. 'The Defence Budget Controversy', *Challenge*, May/June, 1980, (p. 43).

9. G. Prins (ed.), *Defended to Death*, Penguin Books, Harmondsworth, 1983, (p. 179).

10. Ibid. p. 194.

11. Ibid. p. 106.

## Notes to Chapter 6

1. P. R. Webber, 'The Global Effects of Nuclear War', *Science Now*, no. 50, 1983.

2. Y. Laulan, 'Economic Consequences: Back to the Dark Ages',

*Ambio* (Journal of the Royal Swedish Academy of Sciences), vol. 11, no. 2–3, 1982, (p. 149).

3. The Brandt Commission, *Common Crisis: North–South Cooperation for World Recovery*, Pan Books, London, 1983.

4. T. Gervasi, *The Arsenal of Democracy II*, Grove Press, New York, 1981, (p. 207).

5. R. L. Sivard, 'World Military and Social Expenditures', World Priorities, Leesburg, Virginia, 1981.

6. M. Kidron and D. Smith, 'The Arms Sellers', in *The War Atlas: Armed Conflict – Armed Peace*, Pan Books, London, 1983.

7. J. A. Joyce, *The War Machine*, Hamlyn, London, 1981, (p. 136).

8. M. Kidron and R. Segal, 'The Public and the Private', in *The State of the World Atlas*, Pan Books, London, 1981.

9. Technology Transfer Society and Technical Marketing Society of America, *Tactical Missiles for the '90s*, Conference literature, Royal Aeronautical Society, 1981. Also: Technical Marketing Society of America, *The Next Five Years in the US Defence Market*, Conference literature, Royal Aeronautical Society, 1981.

10. S. Zuckerman, *Nuclear Illusion and Reality*, Collins, London, 1982.

11. B. Easlea, *Fathering the Unthinkable – Masculinity, Scientists and the Nuclear Arms Race*, Pluto Press, London, 1983, (p. 165).

## Notes to Chapter 7

1. R. Forsberg, 'A Bilateral Nuclear Weapon Freeze', *Scientific American*, vol. 247, November 1982, (pp. 32–41).

2. L. Aspin, 'The Verification of the SALT-II Agreement', *Scientific American*, vol. 240, February 1979, (pp. 38–45).

3. United Nations, *International Satellite Monitoring Agency: A Proposal*, Disarmament Fact-sheet no. 25, UN, New York, 1982.

4. The Independent Commission on Disarmament and Security Issues, *Common Security*, Pan Books, London, 1982.

5. W. Epstein, 'A Ban on the Production of Fissionable Material for Weapons', *Scientific American*, vol. 243, July 1980, (pp. 43–51).

6. Quoted in: *The Psychology of Nonviolence*, Peace Pledge Union, London, 1982, (p. 6).

7. Ibid. p. 7.

## Notes to Appendix 1

1. SIPRI, *The arms race and arms control*, Taylor & Francis, London, 1982, (p. 85).
2. *Nuclear Weapons*, Report of the UN Secretary General, Autumn Books, Brookline, Mass., 1980, p. 32.
3. F. Barnaby, 'Bombed out of their brains', *Guardian*, 2 December 1982.
4. SIPRI, *The arms race and arms control*, Taylor & Francis, London, 1982, (p. 121).
5. Ibid. p. 87.
6. Ibid. p. 148.
7. SIPRI, *World armaments and disarmament, Yearbook 1977*, Taylor & Francis, London, 1977. See also N. Gardner and A. Harrison, 'Political perspectives on remote sensing', in *Matching Remote Sensing Technologies and their Applications*, Remote Sensing Society, London, 1981.
8. K. Tsipis, 'Cruise missiles', *Scientific American*, vol. 236, February 1977, (p. 20).
9. 'Tiger team keeps missiles on target'. *Observer*, 21 November 1982.
10. SIPRI, *The arms race and arms control*, Taylor & Francis, London, 1982, (p. 146).

## Notes to Appendix 2

1. J. Parmentola and K. Tsipis, 'Particle Beam Weapons', *Scientific American*, vol. 240, April 1979, (pp. 54–65). K. Tsipis, 'Laser Weapons', *Scientific American*, vol. 245, December 1981, (pp. 51–7).
2. F. Barnaby, 'Holocaust by Computer', *Guardian*, 27 January 1983.

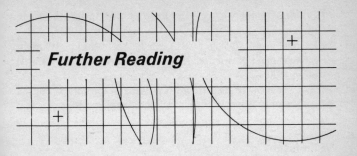

# Further Reading

## Cruise missiles

R. K. Betts (ed.), *Cruise Missiles, Technology, Strategy, Politics*, Brookings Institution, Washington D.C., 1981.

K. Tsipis, *Cruise Missiles, Scientific American* Off-print no. 691, W. H. Freeman, San Francisco, 1977.

## The arms race, nuclear weapons, numbers etc.

Stockholm International Peace Research Institute, *The Arms Race and Arms Control*, Taylor & Francis, London, 1982.

United Nations, *Nuclear Weapons – Report of the UN General Secretary*, Autumn Press, Brookline, Massachusetts, 1980.

Radical Statistics Nuclear Disarmament Group, *The Nuclear Numbers Game*, London, 1982.

G. Prins (ed.), *Defended to Death*, Penguin, Harmondsworth, 1982.

## The effects of nuclear war

O. Greene, B. Rubin, N. Turok, P. Webber and G. Wilkinson, *London After the Bomb*, Oxford University Press, Oxford, 1982.

E. Chivian, S. Chivian, R. J. Lifton and J. E. Mack (eds.), *Last Aid – the Medical Dimensions of Nuclear War*, W. H. Freeman, San Francisco, 1982.

E. Ishikawa and D. L. Swain (trans.), *Hiroshima and Nagasaki – the*

*Physical, Medical, and Social Effects of the Atomic Bombings*, Hutchinson, London, 1981.

S. Glasstone and P. J. Dolan (eds.), *The Effects of Nuclear Weapons*, US Department of Defense and US Department of Energy, Castle House, 1980.

Office of Technology Assessment (Congress of the United States), *The Effects of Nuclear War*, Croom Helm, London, 1980.

## Wider issues

C. Aubrey (ed.), *Nukespeak: The Media and the Bomb*, Comedia Publishing Group, London, 1982.

The Independent Commission on Disarmament and Security Issues, *Common Security: A Programme for Disarmament*, Pan Books, London, 1982.

The Brandt Commission, *Common Crisis*, Pan Books, London, 1983.

J. Rotblat (ed.), *Scientists, the Arms Race and Disarmament*, UNESCO/ Taylor & Francis, London, 1982.

N. Chomsky, J. Steele and J. Gittings, *Superpowers in Collision*, Penguin, Harmondsworth, 1982.

B. Easlea, *Fathering the Unthinkable – Masculinity, Scientists and the Nuclear Arms Race*, Pluto Press, London, 1983.

M. Carver, *A Policy for Peace*, Faber & Faber, London, 1982.

E. Thompson *et al.*, *Exterminism and Cold War*, Verso, London, 1982.

P. Russell, *The Awakening Earth – Our Next Evolutionary Leap*, Routledge & Kegan Paul, London, 1982.

Ken Keyes Jr, *The Hundredth Monkey*, Vision Books, Kentucky, 1981.

M. Kidron and D. Smith, *The War Atlas: Armed Peace – Armed Conflict*, Pan Books, London, 1983.

The Alternative Defence Commission, *Defence without the Bomb*, Taylor & Francis, London, 1983.

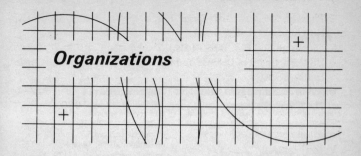

# Organizations

Architects for Peace, 41 St James Road, Sevenoaks, Kent.

Campaign Against the Arms Trade, 5 Caledonian Road, London N1.

Campaign for Nuclear Disarmament (CND), 11 Goodwin Street, London N4.

Center for Defense Information, 303 Capitol Gallery West, 600 Maryland Avenue SW, Washington D.C. 20024, USA.

Civil Engineers for Nuclear Disarmament, c/o 31 Sandbeck Place, Sheffield S11 8XP.

European Nuclear Disarmament (END), 227 Seven Sisters Road, London N7.

Friends of the Earth, 9 Poland Street, London W1.

Journalists Against Nuclear Extermination (JANE), c/o Flat 8, 11 Frognal, London NW3.

Medical Association for Prevention of War (MAPW), c/o 31 Ridings Avenue, London N21.

Medical Campaign Against Nuclear Weapons (MCANW), 23A Tenison Road, Cambridge.

Nursing Campaign Against Nuclear Weapons, 11 Charlotte Street, Bristol 1.

Peace Pledge Union, 6 Endsleigh Street, London WC1.

Schools Against the Bomb, c/o 11 Goodwin Street, London N4.

Scientists Against Nuclear Arms (SANA), 112 Newport Road, New Bradwell, Milton Keynes, MK13 0AA.

Teachers for Peace, 42 York Rise, London NW5.

United Nations Association (UNA), 3 Whitehall Court, London SW1.

World Disarmament Campaign (WDC), 238 Camden Road, London NW1.

# Index